# Once in a Lifetime

Barbara Fisk

Word Art Publishing
9350 Wilshire Blvd
Suite 203, Beverly Hills, CA 90212
www.wordartpublishing.com
Phone: 1 (888) 614 - 1370

Text and Photographs © 2021 Barbara Fisk. All rights reserved.

No part of this book may be reproduced, stored in a retrieval system, or transmitted by any means without the written permission of the author.

Published by Word Art Publishing

ISBN:   Paperback    978-1-955070-02-7
        Hardback     978-1-955070-25-6
        Ebook        978-1-955070-03-4

The line art illustrations on pages 2,3,11,12,16,19,36,47,63,67,69,71,74,86,87,90 and 93 are licensed under the Creative Commons CC0 1.0 license and are in the public domain. Individual attributions are as follows:

Animal illustrations on pages 2,3,11,12,19,36,67,69,71,were donated by Pearson Scott Foresman to Wikimedia Commons, https://commons.wikimedia.org/wiki/Main_Page and are in the public domain. See also papadishu, www.openclipart.org. Butterfly illustration on pages 16,97,98, from A.S. Packard, Jr.'s 1873 book "Our Common Insects," http://www.reusableart.com/butterfly-01.html Page 47: Black Capped Chickadee by Tom Kelley, US Fish & Wildlife Service, http://www.fws.gov/pictures/lineart/tomkelley/blackcappedchickedee.html
Page 63, "Running Dog," from 'Pictures from Dickens with readings', 1895. See Firkin, https://openclipart.org/detail/223215/running-dog Page 74: SnowFlake04 By Doc46, https://openclipart.org/detail/268022/snowflake04
Page 86: Golden Gate Bridge Woodcut by jon phillips https://www.kisscc0.com/clipart/golden-gate-bridge-lynn-canyon-suspension- bridge-c-io49mc/ Page 87: Starfish By johnny_automatic from Lessons in Zoology by Clarabel Gilman, Common Animal Forms, New England Pub. Co prior to 1911 https://openclipart.org/detail/22835/star-fish Page 90: Vintage Victorian Birdcage from PDP, https://www.iconspng.com/image/43297/vintage- victorian-birdcage# Page 93: Single Engine Airplane graphic by spacefem https://openclipart.org/detail/274993/single-engine-airplane

# DEDICATION

This book is dedicated to Kim
Gone so long ago.

# CONTENTS

|   | Introduction | i |
|---|---|---|
| 1 | Reflections of Spring | 1 |
| 2 | Scenes of Summer | 13 |
| 3 | Big Time Bear | 27 |
| 4 | Memories of Autumn | 46 |
| 5 | All the Dogs of My Life | 52 |
| 6 | Wilderness Adventures | 66 |
| 7 | By Land, Sea and Air | 79 |
|   | Afterword | 96 |
|   | About the Author | 99 |

ACKNOWLEDGMENTS

Of all the good things that have happened in my life, the best of all was meeting my future husband, Orville Fisk, when he was on his way to join the Navy. Thanks to him, there is always a new adventure awaiting!

I would also like to thank my parents, Helen and Lenord Pettit, for their gift to me of classical music. My father had a Master's degree in music, and my mother taught piano. Growing up, I learned to play this instrument and others as well. My opportunities to witness and my ability to appreciate the artistry of such favorite great performers as Itzhak Perlman, Arthur Rubinstein and so many others, were a direct result of this gift.

My cousin's son, Patrick Bohanan, started piano lessons as a boy and became interested in the interpretation of Rachmaninoff. Later he became a music teacher and made instructional recordings, and he thoughtfully sent me one of these. My favorite performance of his is "Flight of the Bumblebee." I can see the bee in my mind as he performs this classic. I always admire perfection, and am thankful for his gift.

Finally, I want to thank my friend Kellie Wallace for all the work she put into this book. Without her computer skills, it might never have been published.

# INTRODUCTION

When the stress of daily living or of family and financial burdens occupy all thought to the point where there is no joy in life, one must seek escape in the realm of memory, where no one else may enter to destroy the peace and beauty therein. There one can create a "secret garden" of the mind which enfolds all one's memories of the things that have brought beauty, joy or delight, in moments captured throughout a lifetime.

It has been my fortune to have spent much of my life in the outdoors, and this has resulted in my having many unique sightings of the animals and birds who live there. Often they have remarkable ways of problem solving and expressing themselves through their songs and actions. Hopefully the following little moments I have captured in my own garden of the mind will bring pleasure to all who read them.

# 1: REFLECTIONS OF SPRING

### The White Deer

Early one morning while on a camping trip to the state park near Dry Falls in Eastern Washington, I felt badly after a sleepless night. At last I got up and dressed. It was refreshing to slip out into the clean cool air, filled with the scent of sage, an odor unique to the high desert. The moon and stars were bright, creating light in the dark campground. As I looked through time to the east, the twinkling lights on the horizon were dimmed by the arrival of dawn.

Walking past the huge mulberry trees and out to the edge of the lawn, I noticed movement on the nearby hills. I had an eerie feeling there was something present, and it appeared as pale ghosts slowly approaching. The floating white things held me transfixed with fascination as the early light over the cliffs above the park began to give form to the unreal scene. Sensing the tingle of my hair raising and my heart beginning to pound, I was about to panic and run back to the camper when the light revealed a small herd of white deer, picking their way silently across the lawn and down through the willows which concealed a small stream.

The stars winked out as the rising sun transformed the sky into an ever-changing array of hues, from pale blue to pink, lavender, peach, and then a brilliant flash of orange just before the sunlight's liquid gold slipped over the hills and down the canyon walls. The red clay cliffs leaped from the shadows, the birds began to sing, and even the grass and sage seemed to worship the new day.

## The Birds

I live with my husband on a 110-acre ranch surrounded by trees and pasture. We have many different kinds of birds here-- crows, ravens, eagles, hawks, and in the summer, buzzards. One year, over a span of several months, we would regularly see an eagle sail by our house while flying lower than usual. Then he would return to the tall trees south of our view. One day we were down in a clearing gathering the last of our winter wood, when here came the eagle again! He soared overhead, then made a sharp midair turn and dived straight down to a dead alder tree. With the full weight of the dive behind him, he grabbed a branch in his claws. It broke off and away he flew, in the same direction he had gone so many times before. I was later informed that the eagles start building their nests in the winter so they are ready for a new family in the spring, and that was apparently just what this eagle had been doing.

## The Noisy Blue Jay

Blue jays are one of our most remarkable birds. Clever in attaining what they want, they will work persistently on a problem, trying different ways to solve it.

We feed the birds on our deck daily, and most of the time the food is gone by morning. Once we had been gone all day, and arrived home very late. We tried to sleep in the next morning, but it was not to be. My dreams slowly dissolved with the repeated squawking of a jay by the bedroom window. Becoming impatient with the lack of our response to his wake-up call, he hopped up on the board above the window and began tapping on it. At intervals he would pause and peek over the edge to see if there were any results. Finally, when all else failed, he hopped onto the stone next to the window, clinging tightly to it, and leaned to tap several times on the glass. I lay still and watched while he really put an effort into noise-making, banging as hard as he could with his bill! I tried to quietly wake my husband for him to see this display, but he moved too suddenly and the jay flew up into the nearby maple tree, satisfied that his breakfast would soon follow.

Barbara Fisk

# Better Greedy than Needy

The large deck alongside our house is the perfect place to feed the birds. One day I put out a slice of stale bread broken into small pieces, and one blue jay wanted it all. He kept picking up pieces until he could not stuff anymore into his bill, then flew with it down to a small bank in front of the house. There he carefully laid all the bread down and began preparing a hiding place for it, picking a place clean, then making a small hole. Finally he placed all the bread in it and began to cover it up with dead maple leaves and sticks. Hopping around it several times, he added a few more leaves and flew off to see if any bread was left on the deck; but as soon as he was gone, another jay swooped down from the fir tree above, picked off the leaves and ate the stash!

Few people have heard the blue jays sing their spring mating songs. Usually all one hears from them is a loud, irritating squawking when they are disturbed, or when humans are present. They resemble mockingbirds in that they imitate other birds' songs in a muted manner. They can even sound like little sparrows, chirping and whistling with intermittent clicking of their bills. But if they see a human, they give a loud squawk and fly away!

The feed on the deck attracts all manner of birds, including the watchful eyes of small sparrow hawks. One morning I heard a blue jay screaming in panic and looked down from the deck to see that a hawk had caught one. The hawk was sitting in a low bush, holding his prey with one claw while the Jay was flapping a wing and squawking in panic. I rushed down the stairs and frightened the hawk so it released the jay. Pleased with my rescue, I watched the two birds fly off in different directions.

A few days later the hawk was back, and this time he was not going to be cheated of his catch. When he caught another jay, he flew with it down to the edge of our pond near the house. Landing in the shallow water, he drowned the hapless bird. With no one to intercept his breakfast, he flew off with his prize.

We sometimes put chicken scratch in the shallows along the edge of the pond for the wild ducks. When we put it on the shore the jays ate all of it, so after that it went in the water. One jay, not to be foiled, waded out and fished it from the water, not minding having to duck his head for it.

## Reflections of Nature

As seen from the outside of our house, the windows reflect nearby objects. At times different birds will see their own image and think it is another bird. One spring a song sparrow saw a piece of drift wood with a little nest on it which I had put in the basement window. He spent more than a month courting his own reflection in that window, hopping back and forth on the sill and pecking on the glass. Whenever he tired of his futile pursuit, he would sit in a bush near the window and sing instead.

During the passing seasons, there were other birds who found their own reflections just as attractive. A snowbird, a robin and a peacock all emulated the song sparrow. Just last spring a beautiful oriole had a different reaction entirely. Every morning when the light fell just right on my bedroom window, he would attack the pane, pecking and flapping his wings against it, thinking it was another male invading his territory. Sleep was impossible, and I finally resorted to shutting the drape before I went to bed each night. Triumphant in finally driving his imaginary rival away, he rewarded me with his lovely singing for the rest of the season.

There are so many different kinds of birds that come to the feeders and deck to eat, and those that eat bugs from the tree trunks and bushes nearby. One little bird, a jenny wren, lived in the carport near the house. After a time he became used to us and started coming into the garage. He would sit up on a high perch, safe from harm. One day he sang a sweet little song, so we thought he should have a reward and brought some meal worms we feed to the goldfish. We put some of these out on a flat board covering a dog food bin. As soon as we backed away, he flew down and claimed his prize. It soon became a daily routine for him to sing his little song and be rewarded with a free meal.

## The Wild Ducks

My husband and I put up three wood duck houses in the trees near the pond, which usually attract several pairs of ducks during the spring. Every year before nesting season, we clean out these houses and replace the old wood chip bedding. One spring we found six abandoned eggs from last year's nesting season. Not wanting to waste anything, we put them out on the grass near the pond and the raccoons enjoyed an egg roll! All of the eggs were gone the next morning, except one which had been cracked and eaten on the spot.

Walking by the pond one morning, I spotted half an egg shell in the water and wondered where it came from. Looking out the kitchen window the next day, I saw a wood duck waddling along the shore, carrying a large object in its bill. She waded into the shallow water and began pecking at it. Taking the field glasses for a closer look, I saw it was another egg. As I watched, the duck pounded at it until it finally sank to the bottom. Satisfied, she flew

back up to one of the duck houses. She must have been cleaning up some eggs another duck had left.

Our reward for building those houses and feeding the wild ducks year round is to see the new baby ducks which hatch in the spring. Bright yellow balls of fluff, they dart along the shore and splash in circles, looking for bugs on the water. They are never still, buzzing around like bees after sweet flowers, but in a few days they are gone. Their mothers take them into the creek that feeds the pond and they float from there down to the larger stream, which in turn runs into the nearby salt water bay.

## The Wisdom of the Owls

Owls have always been a a source of fascination to me. One time we were attracted to the noise of different birds hounding an intruder in the trees behind the house. There we saw a great horned owl surrounded by squawking robins, blue jays, and many other small birds. Some made flying passes at the owl, who sat largely ignoring them, only turning his head once in a while to watch them with wide yellow eyes which blinked occasionally when one flew too close. A daring little hummingbird buzzed him several times, then hung suspended in mid-air for a moment close to his watching eyes. The birds annoyed the owl until he finally flew up into a higher tree. There he rested for only a few seconds before he suddenly swooped down to the grass. Catching a large garter snake, he flew away with it dangling from one claw.

I have followed the sound of protesting birds to see owls, eagles, and crows, all of which like to raid the nests of smaller birds. One warm spring night we heard a large owl hooting near the house. It was a low pitched sound, and in moments an answering hoot in a slightly higher pitch replied. They called back and forth for almost an hour. Often on summer evenings we hear the owls calling, large and small, some loud and others soft, usually answered by their own kind.

The evenings hold infinite variety. Colorful sunsets; a robin perched in the highest tree, singing the last song of the day. A doe and fawn slipping from the woods to feed in the approaching moonlight. Frogs announcing spring from their ponds, while the moonlight slips through the trees; and, as I have said, owls exchanging hoots.

There have been several owls which have collided with our windows and been successfully rescued. By bringing them into the house and keeping them in a warm covered cage, we have managed to revive them. One little pygmy was tiny, but he was not going to let our presence scare him! Every time we passed the cage he would ruffle his feathers and click his bill in warning. I kept another owl for several days while he healed, feeding him little bits of raw meat and moths caught by the windows at night. It was always gratifying to see them fly away after they recovered.

## Dance of the Pheasants

Several years ago in springtime, someone released some pheasants near our place. They seemed to be accustomed to people, so we started feeding them, first in the yard, then on the deck. Two pair soon started courting rituals. One brightly colored male was attracted to a little female who was picking away at the grain on the deck. He strutted around her several times. Seeing that she was unimpressed, he tipped his back to one side, slightly spreading his tail and wings, then circled her again with exaggerated, high steps, showing off his brilliant colors. He leaned so far to the side, we thought he was going to tip over! He bobbed his head up and down and strutted around until she ceased her meal and flew down to land near the bushes by the creek.

Following persistently, the male landed by her, but she walked away from him around a bush. Every time he would catch up to her, she would run around to the other side. She seemed to delight in going around and around the bush with the male following. Finally, in a brilliant maneuver, the male turned in the opposite direction. Pausing a moment, he waited for her to disappear, then met her suddenly face-to-face coming around the other side! Surprised, she fluffed her feathers, pecked the grass, then coyly looked at him. The fun of the chase over, they slowly walked away into the woods.

The little hen made her nest in a blackberry thicket down in the nearby pasture, which we could see from the house. While she was nesting, the male pheasant stood on a little knoll keeping watch. One morning a deer and her twin fawns happened upon the scene. One little fawn was so curious about the big bird he kept going closer, pausing between steps-- staring, then advancing again; but the pheasant, king of the knoll, was not going to give ground! When the two were quite close, the fawn stretched his neck forward, as did the pheasant. It appeared as if they almost touched. Satisfied, the little fawn turned to make a quick dash at its twin, and off they went in a game of chase, leaving the pheasant still cock of the walk on his little knoll.

In late summer we separated out several cows to be grained for market. The pheasants soon discovered there was grain left in the wooden feeders and came twice a day to eat with the cows. My husband made a few separate piles for them, and they came while the cows were eating. Otherwise, flocks of crows and ravens would do the cleanup work.

## The Music of Spring

Spring fosters songs from all kinds of creatures, but especially the birds-- most birds never caring if humans see and hear them while so occupied. The crows, however, do not like to share their music, and few people have ever heard a crow sing a spring courting song. Most only hear the loud raucous cawing whenever humans appear, or if the birds are otherwise disturbed. Only once in my lifetime have I heard such a delight, and it was truly a gift from heaven.

It happened one warm spring morning while I was walking my dog along the creek, where huge firs and alders grow. As I walked, I was keenly aware of the scents and sounds of nature: the murmur of the creek, the bees, the smell of the new green grass and wild roses. Suddenly I heard a loud caw, then a funny sound like *clop*, followed by a lovely song, like that of a tiny bird, which seemed to emulate a combination of songs of other birds. Little trills, whistles, and chirps like a canary softly warbling, finally ending with a low *caw*. Then the whole sequence resumed, beginning again with the funny *clop* sound. I lingered there a long time listening, until my dog tugged impatiently at the leash; but as soon as I started walking out into the open, the crow spotted me from his high perch in the big fir tree. When he realized a human had intruded on his private courtship, he flew away, cawing his irritation.

One spring my husband was down in the pasture going to get wood from a dead maple tree. He stopped to take down the electric fence and left the truck door open, and a young crow flew down and landed on the door. He talked to it and put out his arm, and the crow stepped on. There was a little grain left in a bucket, which he scooped up and fed to it. Someone must have raised it from a baby, as the bird obviously remembered people taking care of it. The same thing happened to me when I was walking up the hill from the barn later. When I paused at the top to rest, I saw a crow land in the top of an alder tree. I started talking to it and was surprised to see it fly down and land right at my feet. I kept talking to it but did not have any food, and soon away it went!

One day after I had been shopping at a large market and was returning to the car, I saw that someone had left a can of pop on the sidewalk. A crow spotted it and flew down to check it out. He pecked at it several times, then flipped it over and proceeded to drink the pop as it flowed out of the can. So many birds and animals are problem solvers, and they have so many ways of communicating!

One day I saw three downy woodpeckers on a big cedar log, tapping on the log all at one time. Were they talking to each other, or making bird music?

## 2: SCENES OF SUMMER

### Crows and Ravens

Crows are the clowns of the bird world. They love to play games with each other, or with some object they have found. I have watched some drop an object in mid-air, then dive down below it and catch it again. Sometimes other crows will beat them to it! Some will fly upside down for a second and then flip back upright, and others demonstrate different kinds of aerobatics. They gather in flocks when the light begins to fade, and fly off to roost together for the night.

Crows are almost always the first to sound the alarm if there is an intruder in the area. If an eagle or hawk invades their territory, they will band together and make swooping passes or peck it on the back or head, all the while cawing and annoying the stranger until they finally drive it away.

There is always something new occurring in nature. This time we were working at pulling noxious weeds in one of the pastures when a big raven landed to sit in a large fir tree near the edge of the field. It began to talk in raven language, and when I tried to mimic, it flew away. The next time my husband went down to feed the cows, he took a slice of bread and left it by the feeder pan for the coyotes. As soon as he drove away, that raven swooped down and got his prize! From then on, it was repeated every day. Sometimes the big bird even brought a friend and had to share! So now we have a pet raven.

We put out old bread, scraps, fat and bones from our butchering for the birds and coyotes. The banquet attracts eagles, buzzards, ravens and crows, all competing for the food. One day while the crows were pecking on chunks of fat, their squabbling attracted one of our young calves. When the curious calf came close, all the birds flew away except for one particularly bold and hungry one. It flew up onto a big old tree stump nearby. As soon as the calf lost interest, the crow flew down to resume eating, only to have the calf quickly chase it back to the safety of the stump again. Every time the crow landed by the fat, the calf would come back and chase it to the stump! The sequence evolved into a game, until the crow finally gave up and flew away.

These shiny black birds are constant inhabitants of the state and national parks, attracted by free handouts from campers. On one occasion when I was at a park, I witnessed a group of children gathered around a picnic table, their attention focused on something. Three adults went over to see what was taking place, and found one boy had a stick, and was poking at a huge, newly hatched moth. The adults urged the children to just watch, and not bother it.

The moth had just emerged from the confines of its cocoon. The bright spring sun filtered through the huge cedar trees, creating a warm spot on the table, which helped the wings of the moth slowly begin to unfold and dry. The group gathered at the table did not see the pair of shiny black eyes in the tree above them also watching the scene. The beautiful moth began to work its wings up and down, readying them for a first flight, and finally took off, soaring up into the air to the delight of all watching. Then disaster struck! The black eyes hidden in the tree were attached to a huge raven which swooped down, snatched the moth in mid-air, and flew away with breakfast.

In nature, there are the quick and the dead.

## Nature Heals

Nature has a way of healing some of the animals who suffer attacks by predators. One morning we saw a doe and a fawn being chased by a coyote. The doe jumped a barbed wire fence, but the little fawn tried to squeeze between two strands and was wounded. A large piece of skin was torn from its back. Realizing that her fawn was in danger, the doe turned and went back over to the fence and chased the coyote away. It took several weeks for the little fawn's wound to begin healing, but with the doe's maternal care, new skin slowly covered the injury and, by fall, fresh hair began to grow.

One time a band of raccoons came up to our house for their evening meal, but upon arriving on the deck, one of them lay down, ignoring the food. It looked like something had taken a huge bite of fur and skin off her back behind her head, leaving a raw place the size of a saucer. Again, nature slowly healed the wound. With the passing of time, new skin gradually formed and finally fur began to grow. The raccoon used the safety of the deck to spend most of her time while nature performed this miracle.

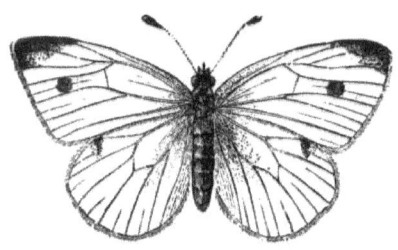

The Butterfly of Hope

There is always a butterfly in life that comes to bring comfort when one is tired and discouraged, physically and mentally, from everyday living. One day I was sitting by the flower bed, weeding and feeling sorry for myself. Several years of a persistent illness had resulted in my neglecting the yard, and working to clear the weeds was painfully difficult. "What is the use? Who cares if there are flowers here?" I thought, dispirited, and let the spade slip to the ground. Life seemed to hold little promise. I was staring through tears at nothing.

Then came a butterfly, floating across the grass to a cluster of bright red flowers, settling on one so close that every detail of its body could be seen. It was a pale yellow, with blue and black spots distinctive of the swallowtail clan. The tiny, fine hairs on its wings, body and head were visible while it drank sweet life from each blossom, seeming to enjoy the warm sun and the nectar in the flower.

Finally satisfied, it flew into the air, and another of its kind appeared. They met in a fluttering dance in the sun. One flew a short distance, followed by the other, then again fluttering together, rising up into the air and then floating down over and over again in a courtship ritual, thus insuring their immortality. Finally they wound their way higher and higher, until, clinging together, they descended to the garden below, their wings making a tiny rustling sound as they disappeared into the green leaves.

The beauty of the scene revived my hopes. With the help of a dear friend, we located a person who really listened to my symptoms and guided me to the right doctor. With all their help my health gradually improved over a long period of time, and the bright butterfly of a new friendship evolved.

## The Fawn's Surprise

Midsummer found our fields and pastures threatened with a takeover by the noxious weed called tansy ragwort, which is poisonous to domestic animals. I had spent part of each day for a week digging and pulling the tough, three-to-four-foot tall plants to keep them from producing millions of seeds. My husband was fishing in Alaska at the time, and I had taken up over five pickup loads with no help. After working in an area of tall grass and bushes for three hours, I thought I had pulled all of the plants. I am not very tall, so I climbed up on a big old-growth tree stump to survey the area. Feeling hot, tired, and sorry for myself, I stood there for a few minutes, rubbing my sore lower back and letting my mind wander. I thought, "I'm not built for this kind of work. If I were rich, I could hire someone to do it!"

The fantasy was appealing. Maybe I could get rich quick by writing a book on *101 Ways to Pull Tansy Ragwort!* First, there was the 'step-over and tug method' using a leg for leverage, or again, there was the 'chopping off the base of the roots with the hoe-and-pull method.' I could sell my book or have Reader's Digest publish it and the money would roll in! Then I shook my head.

"What a stupid idea! How many people even know what tansy ragwort is?"

As I stood on the great stump the pain in my back gradually eased off, and as the beauty of the morning penetrated the dullness of my thoughts, I stopped feeling sorry for myself. The hum of the insects, the birds singing, the sun shining on the grass and trees, the big white fluffy clouds floating in the bright blue sky-- who could witness all this and be unhappy?

Suddenly I was aware of a small cry coming from the nearby thicket of trees and bushes. It sounded like a baby lamb or goat: *maaa, maaa!* It was an urgent, high-toned call. My mothering instincts aroused, I impulsively made an answering call in a soft, lower tone. No one that I knew in the neighborhood had sheep or goats. I thought if I could lure this baby into the open, I might be able to rescue it.

Each time the little creature called I answered. Gradually the sound came closer and closer. Then the grass moved nearby, and a few seconds later a tiny spotted fawn cautiously approached the stump! It gave another little *maaa, maaa* and walked right up, sniffing anxiously. The little fellow sniffed again, then looked suddenly up to see the huge giant "something" standing on top of the stump. Surprise! It was not Mamma who had answered!

A wave of emotion instantly swept across that little face and eyes-- first surprise, then consternation, horror, and fear! He leaped back, wheeled and dashed away to the safety of the thicket.

No one will ever convince me that animals do not have feelings, emotions, and expressions in their faces and eyes! That little fawn may have had an unpleasant surprise, but I had the delight of a wonderful experience which few have ever had. All my hard work pulling weeds had been worth it that day!

In retrospect, I later realized that calling the fawn could have brought the attention of a cougar. That certainly would have been as hazardous and frightening an experience for me, as my presence had been to the fawn!

## Predators and Prey

We have always put out food for all of the wildlife which share our "hundred-acre woods--" raccoons, birds, deer, coyotes and more. The deer have a safe haven here, and every spring new fawns are born. On some occasions there are twins! They have become accustomed to finding apples on the grass below the deck where we throw cut pieces down. One day we saw a buck rubbing the velvet off his horns on a willow tree growing by the creek.

One morning we looked down from our deck and saw that a doe had given birth to a tiny fawn which was struggling to stand. Meanwhile, watching from the woods nearby was a pair of yellow eyes that belonged to a large bobcat. The doe was well aware of this onlooker, and guarded her baby closely until it was strong enough to follow her. Then she slowly led the little one away, all the while keeping it safe from the bobcat.

One warm sunny afternoon when I was coming down the driveway I saw the tall grass by the creek waving around, so I stopped the car and got out, walking over to the bridge. The grass wiggled again, and up popped a bright-eyed little weasel! He looked all around, then dived back down into the grass. This happened several times; he was so busy looking for something in the grass that he did not even glance my way. Finally he stood up again, turning his head this way and that, watching the area near him. As I observed the little drama, a tiny mouse leaped into the creek and, madly paddling, headed for the bank on the other side. It was the only escape route, and the mouse had won this game of hide-and-seek!

One warm summer day I was walking by the pond when a dragonfly lit on my arm. It slowly relaxed its wings and seemed to like the surface it had landed on. Satisfied, it flew up into the air, paused a few seconds, then flew away.

## Animal Families

The raccoons are nightly visitors to our house, and have a feast on the dry dog food we put out. They used to come in the daytime, but a mean man living across the valley kept shooting and poisoning them until very few were left. In the spring the mothers would bring their babies and spend a lot of time on the deck. There was one momma who loved marshmallows. I would hold one out and she would stand on her hind legs and stretch her arms out so I could drop it into her little waiting hands. Another one whom we called "Standing Coon" would stand on his hind legs, put out one arm against the door jamb and lean against it while waiting for his marshmallow. One time I was working below the deck cutting grass and looked up to see a whole row of little faces watching me. I went in, got my camera, and they were still there when I came back, so I have a picture to remember them by.

## Baby Coyotes

Late one afternoon, we came home from town. After closing the gate to our property, we started down the long drive toward home. Suddenly we saw two little half-grown coyote pups by the creek. We slowed down as they dashed into the woods.

We saw the pups several times after that, when we went out the driveway. We could see they had no mother and were slowly starving, so we started putting dry dog food by the path where they came out of the woods. The smallest one did not survive, but the larger one did, and slowly he filled out and began to grow. We called him "Wile E. Coyote" after the cartoon character. Whenever I would see him I would call his name and talk to him. He would stop and listen for a bit, and then go on his way.

Once again our nasty neighbor did his dirty work. He would shoot any time of the day or night, leaving out bait and shining a light so he could kill the coyotes. Over a period of time the pack was destroyed, and how we missed their singing at night! They would even start howling if they heard a fire or police siren. The last time I saw a cub, it was poised above a tall stand of grass, watching and waiting for a mouse to move so he could catch it. When the mother coyote saw me, she came out of the woods. With some kind of signal she got him to come to her, and away they went into the safety of the forest.

Even though most of the coyotes were killed, they had their revenge as rats and mice moved into the town in great quantity, and to this day we know people who are constantly battling their invasion. Still, despite our neighbor, Wile E. survived and found a mate! We saw three young pups last year, and slowly they are beginning to multiply and sing for us again. Whenever we have food scraps, we put them down for the coyotes in a pan, and cover it with a board so the crows will not eat it instead.

## Herding Cows

One summer when Orville had gone fishing in Alaska, I received an early morning wake-up call saying our beef cows were out on the county road headed north. I quickly dressed in jeans and hiking shoes and walked up the road looking for signs of cow pies. The man who had called me saw me there and said they'd gone across the road and up the power line.

I had taken a wooden broomstick as a 'persuader' to influence the cows to return home when I found them. The weather, fortunately, was in my favor—not too hot or too cold. After two hours of walking, I found the herd just beginning to bed down to rest. I got around behind them and began to shout at them and wave my stick. They all started back toward home, and anyone who slowed down got a whack on the back with my broomstick. When we got to the road, instead of crossing it and going down the old logging road to their pasture, the idiots went down the county road instead! The only way they got turned off the road was when a big semi truck stopped in the way and the driver got out and waved his arms at them!

Of course the cows took worst possible cross-country route for me to follow—right through the thick brush and straight across the creek. My broomstick helped some, and finally the pasture fence was in view. I tried to get them to go up to the gate, but they just stood there, so I walked on back to the house and called a friend. I had started out at six in the morning, and it was noon by the time the cattle drive was over. I was exhausted! I took a shower and discovered big blisters on my feet from walking so far. I spend most of that day recuperating from this adventure. The only way I like a cow is as a nice big steak on my dinner plate!

## A True Story, Full of Bull

When we first moved onto our acreage, there were open fields which made perfect pasture, so we bought two beef heifers. Our neighbor had milk cows and a bull, Bruno, that she had raised from a little calf. He was used to her and not aggressive. We wanted to breed our cows, so she loaned him to us. Whenever I would go walking through the pasture, I always took an apple to give him. I would talk to him and call his name.

In late summer his owner wanted to loan him to relatives who had cows to breed. She came over and together we herded him back through the neighbor's field to her property, where a fine new big corral had been built. She got a bucket of grain to give her other cows to keep them busy while I moved Bruno into a smaller pen, where a horse trailer was parked. The eight-foot fence was made of new two-by-six lumber. Atop one section of the fence, several would-be cowboys were perched, safe from the bull.

I held the big gate of the pen to keep Bruno in, but another so-called cowboy waved his arms and shouted "Haah! Haah!" at the bull to force him into the trailer. He was not used to men or this rude treatment, and whirled around looking for an avenue of escape. My eyes were at the level of the top of the gate and suddenly Bruno and I were face to face. The expression in his eyes was one of pure rage. I said, "Bruno," and the rage melted into recognition. He whirled around and with one huge leap cleared the eight foot fence with his front quarters, while his hind legs smashed the heavy top plank as he completed his leap to freedom.

It pays to know your bull, and to talk to the animals.

## Brother Bear

Over the passing years several bears have come to visit us, like the one who found our best apple tree in the orchard and picked and ate all but two of the fruits, which he was nice enough to leave for us! Then there was another tall apple tree just past the barn which was loaded with our supply of winter keepers, but when we went to pick them, there were only a few left on the high branches-- and all around the area there were piles of 'applesauce' which the bear had made after eating all he could hold.

On one walk through the woods, our little dog Scooter spotted a black bear and ran barking to chase him away. Fearing the bear would turn on him, I ran after both of them, screaming at Scooter to stop! Hearing all this noise, the bear ran down the hill and got away as fast as he could. Most bears are not aggressive unless provoked.

We wanted to produce our own honey, so we started with two beehives, and the first year had them down in the apple orchard. Brother Bear found a lovely sweet surprise there, and took one hive apart, eating all the honey. We moved the other hive up behind the house for safekeeping and a few days later saw large tracks in the snow, heading for another treat!

We had a vegetable garden down past the creek and pond, and one day it was time for me to do some weeding there. I headed down the path from the house to the creek, carrying a small bucket of gardening tools. Stopping to admire some of my flowers along the way, I heard the sound of something big moving in the thick brush nearby. The cracking of small branches sent me back up the path to the house again to get a gun. Now armed with a .22 rifle and a .38 pistol, I ventured down the path again, listening for more sounds, but fear took the place of curiosity when I heard larger branches cracking, interspersed with snuffling noises. Playing "chicken little," I found the way back only took a few minutes to navigate! Discretion had taken the better part of valor, but there is always another day to garden.

Years ago I found a little baby black bear who was starving and lost. Some macho hunter had killed her mother and tacked its hide to his garage wall. The story of her life with us is a tale of fun and laughter, and we took many photos as she grew from a starving little baby into a movie star!

## 3: BIG TIME BEAR

April 4, 1969 was a Good Friday, bringing a windy day that pushed the big fluffy white clouds around the sky in a game of chase. The sun peeked in and out between them, with little chance of warming the day.

Our daughter, Cheryl, kept her Arabian horse close to the house as it had given birth to a little colt in late March. We needed some fresh bedding for their shelter, so, armed with shovels and a big wastebasket for scooping, we drove to a small rural farm where the owner had a little sawmill.

I parked the pickup truck close to a large pile of fresh sawdust and began shoveling it. Cheryl stayed in the vehicle, because the sharp wind made it seem much colder than it was. The only pleasant thing about that wind was that it bore the sweet scent of spring flowers, green trees and grass.

While I was working, I glanced up to see the farmer's herd of white faced cattle suddenly bolt and run up to the fence nearby. They stood staring with bulging-eyed bovine stupidity at a small black creature running across the pasture. The mill owner's Siberian Husky ran growling in the direction of the animal until, reaching it, the dog detected the scent of bear and leaped backwards in surprise.

The tiny bear was crying *"Maa! Maa!"* as it ran towards me. Barking and growling, the dog rushed it again, this time being a bit bolder. The bear cub had seen me by then. I was wearing a black sky jacket, dark pants and boots, and it must have thought I was its mother, as it scooted under the fence and right up to me!

The dog was closing in fast, so I grabbed the little cub by the scruff of the neck and held it high in the air, running to the truck. Shooing the dog away and opening the door, I stuffed the little fellow into the sawdust wastebasket, much to Cheryl's surprise! I then had her watch the woods and the pasture to see if she could see a mother bear looking for her cub.

The wind was blowing from the direction of the woods. After awhile the cows drifted back down to the edge of the trees and stood looking around for a bit. Then, seeming to smell no danger, they went back to grazing the fresh spring grass.

It took awhile to finish filling the truck with sawdust, and after I did we prepared to head home. I was certain there was no mother bear nearby, as it surely would have come looking when the baby cried. Besides, I was not about to go carrying it back down all the way to the woods, through a pasture full of big steers, and go hunting for a mother bear with her crying cub in my arms! But our final decision was made when we spied, nailed to the garage wall of the house across the street, a fresh black bear's hide. Some macho hunter must have killed that mother bear. So we took the little cub home.

She was so tiny, only about nine inches tall and fifteen inches long, just beginning to cut her small front teeth! First we had to clean her up with a warm wet cloth, as she was covered with dirt and mud. She must have gone a long time without food, as she was all fur and bones. I warmed some milk, put it into a bowl, and dipped a small cloth in it, holding it so she could suck on the end of it. The minute she began to imbibe some milk, her little stomach began to gurgle and rumble.

Cindy, our little dog, was afraid of her at first, but eventually she took the little bear in tow and went to bed with her. Soon both were asleep. That night we made a special bed in a little box lined with a soft cloth, and put the cub in a cage for the night.

On Saturday morning the little bear woke us up, calling "*Maa! Maa!*" She was as cross as a bear, too, until we gave her a baby bottle full of milk. Then she made little comforting noises as she drank that sounded like a little motor-- *umaaaaaa, munaaaaa.* When she was finished, we took her out on the lawn to do her bear business. She could not do much, as her system must have been completely empty. She didn't make any water for three days.

Our new cub seemed to have a great fear of being left alone, and would run to us and try to climb up our legs to be held close. When she got tired, someone would hold her and sing a little song, rocking her to sleep. She had a lot of fun playing, and would run and tackle someone's feet, chewing their shoe and laces. She tried to climb things, finally finding a place in the furnace room where the dog food bag and boxes were, then clambering up the back wall of the brick fireplace!

In the mornings, the little bear was always very hungry and impatient, making it hard to feed her. She would grab the bottle and rip the nipple out, flooding herself with milk. Since I was not into cleaning up messes, I decided to try and train her like a puppy, and started to take her outside to take care of herself. As soon as she was done, she ran for the back door and wanted back in. She slept with our dog Cindy in the evenings, but at bedtime we continued putting her in her little bed in a large rabbit cage for the night.

A few days after we found her, she developed a runny nose and bad eyes, so I took her to our veterinarian to see what was wrong. The vet had a pet raccoon in a pen outside the office. I thought she needed to see other animals, so I held her up to check out the new critter. They sniffed noses, and the raccoon's expression changed instantly from curiosity to shock, horror and fear. Not wanting to scare him further, we went on into the office. The people who saw her were very surprised, and said they had never seen such a small little bear before. With some medication, she was better in a few days.

During her first week at our house, our bear spent all her time eating, sleeping, and getting into mischief. She took over the dog's bed in the washroom. When awake, she was always looking for something to do. One delight she soon found was unwinding the toilet tissue in the bathroom!

In her second week, she finally learned how to climb the back stairs, and had fun playing with the dog and some of her new toys.

Some of her favorite playthings were a toy stuffed bear, as well as the dog's possessions. Anything new was fun, and had to be checked out. When I had the dishwasher door open, she would climb up and check out the food on the dirty dishes which were ready to be washed.

A game of chase was always great fun too! The cub would always be in the lead, with Cindy trying to catch her. When she was tired and wanted to end the game, she would dive under the davenport. Laying on her back, she would pull herself along with her front feet on the underside of the sofa. She would tease the dog by reaching out from beneath the furniture with a paw, trying to bat her face. Climbing especially was her thing, whether on the recliner, the davenport, or the chairs around the table!

One warm spring day, the little bear and I were gardening out in the back yard when there came the sound of a car driving up in front of the house. I put our bear in the fence around the swimming pool for safety, and Cindy rushed about barking as I followed her around the house. A pleasant lady got out of the car and we began to talk as she admired Cheryl's new little colt in the pasture. Watching the dog and colt sniffing each other, she said it reminded her of a lovely story they were studying, about how the wild animals would come to live in peace together with the tame ones. She was going to give me one of her pamphlets from the Watchtower religious group. She turned to a little booklet and thumbed through it until she found a page with a picture on it depicting this story. Meanwhile, Cindy had lost interest in the colt, and had gone to lay down in the shade.

Suddenly our little bear came running toward us across the lawn, crying her usual *"Maaa! Maaa!"* She had gotten out of the fence! She rushed over to me, then went into the pasture to sniff noses with the colt. The lady and the other strangers in the car were astonished to see that a dog, a bear, and a horse could all live together! Her bible story fell flat when I said, "There is your proof! The lion shall lie down with the lamb!"

As the days passed and she began to grow, our bear did new and different things. We would give her a bath in a big pan, as she liked to play in water. One of her favorite things to do was to play with the garden hose when water was coming out of it. She would feel it with her front paws, using them like hands.

I usually fed our cub her bottle out in the front yard, holding it up so she could grasp it with her front paws, then slowly laying her

down so she could drink it by herself. Whenever she ate, our cub made her usual comforting sound of *ah-uh-uh*.

Eventually I started mixing baby pablum, strained meat, chicken and fruit into her milk, trying to think of what she would be eating in the wild. Several times she went to sleep when drinking her bedtime bottle, with the milk drooling out of her mouth as she had drunk too much. Once I found her laying on her back this way, with her stomach bulging. Suddenly she flipped over on her feet, bit me on the hand, and rushed to the safety of her cage, throwing up all over on her way to the dog bed, where the rest of her dinner landed! She seemed to think it was all my fault!

Every day there was something new. With her clever and agile front paws, she learned to open the kitchen cabinet drawers and climb up them like stairs, up onto the counter so she could reach the cupboards where there was the chance of getting into some food. She was growing stronger by the day. Her feet became huge, and her claws so sharp they had to be trimmed.

Climbing trees became a favorite pastime. She also liked to sit in a chair with Cheryl and Kim while they cuddled and petted her. Once we had some visitors come with their children, who were dressed in red. This color seemed to anger her, and she ran at them trying to chase them away.

One time we took her to the local park for a picnic, and let her walk around with a little dog harness and leash. Few people even noticed she was a bear, as I had black Cindy, and my mother had her little Sidney Silky Tam with her, and, armed with her bottles, she was a very good little bear. We took her to different parks. One park featured a long beach near the saltwater sound. Testing the cold salt water and the things on the beach were of great interest to her. But the next time she went traveling, it was to a horse show, and she was horrible, cross, and did not want to be tied up! Revenge was hers as she made a big mess in the car, and cried her *"Maaa! Maaa!"* all the way going and all the way coming back. Everyone was glad to get home!

Our daughter Cheryl took the cub to school one day, leading her around in a little harness and leash. They toured most of the classes, and for some reason she was a very good little bear. Whenever she got tired and cross, she squeezed up her eyes and laid back her ears, looking really mean and ready to bite anyone in reach. When feeding, if the milk did not come fast enough, it made her angry, and she got even by pulling the nipple out of the bottle.

When we were trying to clean her off with a cloth, she resented it and fidgeted, and whenever anyone left a towel or cloth hanging on a chair, it was fair game to pull it down. Many times she was found asleep on someone's bed. On another occasion, no one could find her! The hunt ended when she was discovered sleeping in the clothes closet.

As the days passed, our cub grew more rapidly, spending most of her time outside, always exploring and checking out new things. A bright yellow dandelion caught her attention and she touched it with her paws, sniffed, and tried tasting it. A large cedar tree on the edge of the yard was her favorite place to spend time. Climbing up to a high branch, she lay on her stomach with her front and hind feet hanging down on each side. One day three black crows saw her and set up a big, cawing fuss. They made flying passes at her, trying to drive her from the tree. Once, when coming down out of her favorite woods, she slid slowly on her belly through the flowers, pulling herself along with her front feet while letting her hind feet drag along with her stomach!

Now the little bear spent most of her days outside in the yard or in the woods, playing with bushes, ferns and grass. One of her pastimes was to climb partway up a tree, release her hold and ride wildly down to the ground, sliding from branch to branch! Another game was to tease us by running at something and slapping at it to see if we would scold or run after her. Once the kids wanted to set up a tent and night camp in the back yard near the woods, but their little buddy kept dashing around them, in and out of the woods, and finally up a tree. She was so full of energy, and not careful about her climbing. Eventually she fell out of the tree, but was not hurt as the brush below broke her fall. The final assault on the children's camp was to leave a big poo in the middle of the plastic they had laid on the ground for the sleeping bags.

As time passed and more people knew we had her, she had many visitors. Some wanted to take her and make a home for her, and many played with her, bringing treats of gumdrops or taffy. On hot days, a special treat of ice cream or sherbet was always welcome.

Another of her favorite foods was applesauce. She liked to play a game of run, charge and wrestle with Kim and my husband Orville, standing on her hind legs and walking like a human with her front arms and paws outstretched, ready to tackle someone!

Our bear liked visitors. When the furnace repairman came, she tried to help him fix it by climbing in and around his legs and arms, and then into his tool box. Exploring and keeping busy was her thing, especially in the children' rooms where there were toys, and Cheryl's pet gerbils and birds. When she saw there was something alive in a cage, she would slap it with her paw several times.

Just outside the back door was a patio, with a stone wall holding up a dirt bank, where sometimes I would put treats. One lovely warm spring morning she climbed the wall and sat on the bank, slowly tipping onto her back, pointing her nose in the air, pushing out her upper lip and sniffing the sweet morning air. Mesmerized by the warm sun and sweet spring air, she slowly drifted off to sleep.

Indoors, our bathtub became an attraction to her after she found she could get into it by making a run and diving headfirst into it! If I was taking a bath at the time, she would lean over the side and slap at the soap foam and bubbles. It was rather hard to find a bear sitter, so after a time I started shutting her in the bathroom with a few toys whenever we had to leave the house for a few hours. One time when we returned, she had done a poo in the bathtub and had proceeded to have fun smearing it all over the tub and walls. Other times she would just go to sleep in the tub. Another of her pleasures was to sit in the hand basin and look into the medicine cabinet mirror. Anything unguarded was fair game.

Sometimes our cub came with us in the car on short trips, but on other days she had to stay home, locked in her cage. Occasionally she managed to open a cupboard door and create a huge mess, or went potty wherever she chose, leaving a big mess to clean up. Every day something different would occur. Once she found a little black feather, and when she came to her bed she laid down and went to sleep with it. Sometimes when she got rather sloppy drinking her milk, she would put her paws up over her mouth and eyes to hide her face from me when I tried to wipe it!

Our family mealtime was a tempting attraction to her. She would climb up on the kitchen chairs looking for something to eat on the table, and wait for a sweet treat. Applesauce was a favorite of hers, as well as licking the jelly spoons.

She liked to be brushed, or scratched under the chin or on the back, which produced a pleased look on her face, with her upper lip pushed out in a smile, it felt so good. We made her a climbing tree out of the top of a cedar, put it on a stand and tied some toys to it. A stocking stuffed with rags was her favorite!

The children, meanwhile, were in 4-H horse groups, and once they left a saddle out on the lawn. This was another challenge for our little bear! She climbed up on it and sat on it like a person, taking hold of the pommel with her hands and rocking back and forth like a little cowboy!

The horse watering trough was another attraction. She would climb into it, splashing around and getting all wet, then suddenly spook and jump out to run around chasing the dog or whoever was wanting to play with her. Most every day I had to clean up some mess she made, and trying to sweep or dust mop was another challenge, as both Cindy and her little bear buddy liked to chase the mop and broom! Still, life does have its compensations-- any time when some visitor came and things were not neat and clean, I could always blame the bear!

Our little town has an annual parade for the children and their pets, so when it was time, we tied our bear cage to the kids' little red wagon and hung a sign on it saying, "Peace, Don't Shoot Mother Bears!" Kim dressed up like a hippie with a straw hat and a gunny sack for a shirt. Cindy went along too on a leash as he pulled the wagon in a peace protest against killing bears. They won the first place prize!

Our little bear was the very personification of the phrase "perpetual motion." She was always playing, and exploring new things with her paws-- flowers, grass and trees. One time she came in with grass pasted to the end of her nose. She had found out what those funny black things were that came slowly sliding across the ground. Slug slime had gotten stuck to her nose, and she'd been trying to rub it off in the grass!

Sometimes she would get to ride with us in the car, whenever possible. One hot day she began to get cross as we drove, probably too hot in her fur coat. Arriving home, she was so glad to be back in her own yard that she ran around it, then jumped into the horse trough, then out again to dash madly from tree to tree, climbing a little ways up, then backing down to run to the next one and do the same thing over again! Finally she ended up on a high branch, where she went to sleep for around two hours.

One time, things became too quiet, and I went looking for my little baby. Someone had made the mistake of leaving the toilet lid up. When I found her, she had both paws in the toilet, stirring the water around. I stood quietly watching until she looked up, saw me, and leaped into the bathtub! When she got out of the bathtub she slid on her stomach, letting her hind feet stretch out behind until she slowly slid onto the floor. I closed the door and she ran around the bathroom, spreading wet paw tracks over everything-- another mess to clean up. The house looked like a disaster at times that spring, as my house cleaning went to pot. I told myself I would try again next year!

One cool, cloudy day my little bear did not go out, and instead was a constant distraction while I tried to do my morning chores of sweeping and mopping. She tackled everything that moved, including my feet. Suddenly nature stopped the fun when she had to go potty, and she started to go on the floor! I grabbed her up and headed for the back door, but the 'go button' would not turn off and she went poo all the way to the back door, and all over the rug, my slacks, socks and shoes! Score one for the bear, zero for Mom. Finishing outside, she then climbed to the top of a forty-foot cedar tree for a quick, safe retreat!

When our bear wanted in through the back screen door, she found a clever way to open it by first pulling it partway open, then hooking her claws around the edge and walking around it on her hind feet and so on into the house. She liked to play with Orville, batting at him with her front feet. One evening after a fun game, she ran into the bathroom to get a drink out of the dripping faucet in the tub. I had her bedtime bottle ready, and when I called her, she crawled to the front end of the tub and dragged herself out in a slow, flowing motion, letting her hind feet trail out behind like a frog's. The warm bottle ended the day.

Time went by so quickly, until we had had our little bear for over a month. Gradually she had been growing and changing, and now she weighed a whole 15 pounds!

Every day brought new challenges. Once I could not find my little gardening shovel and thought it was lost. Then, a week later, I found it hidden behind the stone wall on the patio!

Tree climbing, as I have said, was one of her favorite things, and our house was surrounded by them. A fifty-footer lured her up to near the top as a windstorm was blowing the branches around, causing the tree to sway and giving her a free ride while she played with the swinging branches. She liked to take naps on the bigger limbs, and one time she must have chosen the wrong tree as a robin flew at her and stood on a branch scolding her until she left!

Indoors, we made our bedrooms off limits, and we kept the hall door closed. Whenever I forgot, she would go in and play or sleep on the beds. I missed her one day and went looking for her, and there she was sitting on my bed, looking so cute I could not scold her.

Running water into the bathtub was always an attraction, and watching the bubbles rising up got her so excited that she fell in! One big leap and she was out again, running into Kim's bedroom and jumping up on the bed, getting it all wet.

There were times when we had to be gone most of the day, and then we would ask a friend to let her out of her cage to eat and drink. Once, when he put her back in the cage, the latch did not hold, and disaster ensued. We came home to find my sweet little bear had taken the kitchen apart! Making stairs out of the drawers had gained her access to the cupboards and canisters, and nuts were scattered all over the counter! My favorite little hand-painted vase was broken, and a box of plants was tipped over and the dirt all tracked around in the sink and over the counter tops. The curtain tie-backs were ripped down. Those clever little front paws had opened the cupboards, and a big jar of candy had been found and almost every piece tasted! The doors under the sink had been opened too, and another prize, a bag of trash, had been scattered all over the floor. And all that fun had ended with a pile of poo on the floor!

At least we had remembered to close Cheryl's bedroom and hall door, and that was good, for, looking for more to do, our cub had climbed up into the bathroom sink and pulled down the electric toothbrushes and the soap dish. Leaving no object intact, she had cleared all the papers and phones off the desk by the window. After we got home, that naughty little bear was spooked up the rest of the day, and kept tackling the dog when they were outside playing in the back yard.

Each day our little cub learned something new and became smarter. A good game was to hang onto the backyard swing seat, swinging around and batting at the dog. Trying to climb the chain link fence around the swimming pool was a failure, so it turned into another game of tease-and-chase with Cindy. Nothing seemed to slow that little bear down! She would think up new ways to do something she knew she was not supposed to do, and then run and climb a tree to get away when we chased her. A bicycle left out was another temptation. Looking around to see if anyone was watching, she ran over to it, looked around again, then pushed it over and dashed off to the safety of the closest tree! There was always some daily mess to clean up; she would play out in the horse pasture by the water tub, and then come into the kitchen and run across the floor, leaving a trail of muddy footprints.

I knew the time would come when a new home would have to be found for our little bear, but it came sooner than I thought. The state made a new law declaring that black bears were to be designated game animals, so it would be illegal for us to try to keep her any longer. I wrote a letter to Walt Disney to see if they could take her and use her in some of their movies, but California had the same law as the new one in Washington State. They suggested trying the Olympic Game Farm in Sequim, which rescued injured game animals. I contacted the State Department of Fish and Game to try to enlist their help. They said they had another little bear cub at their facility in Tacoma, and that they would come and get our cub. I thought they would have a better chance at finding a home for her than I would.

The State officer came a few days later in a station wagon with a wooden box in the back. I was so angry when he stuffed my precious little friend into that box and put a padlock on it! The day ended in tears, and there was a lump in my throat when I went into the house and saw her toys lying where she had left them, the stuffed sock still hanging soggily from the play fir tree branch. How she had loved to run and tackle it! My trampled flower beds would grow back by next spring, and I could replant my tuberous begonias, which had ended up sitting on the bow of Orville's boat for a month, out of the way of busy paws. The ferns and flowers would all come back, but there would never be another little bear in my life.

But no one can take away my memories. All the hard work I did, and all the messes I cleaned up, would fade from my mind with time, but never my little bear. I gave her the best time of her life, with plenty of food, freedom, love and care. It was a terrible thought to know she would be confined for the rest of her life, never to roam the woods or to slip quietly among the green ferns and flowers to her little hideaway. The only consolation was that she had gone to keep another little lonesome, crying bear cub company, and that no hunters would take her life.

I kept in contact with Fish and Game to see if they could place her in a zoo or some other facility. On my last call I was informed that they had placed the first little bear, but if they could not soon find a place for my little bear, they would have to euthanize her, as they could not turn her out into the wild. I told the officer to not even consider such a thing, and to find a place for my bear or I would contact a TV reporter, bring him down there with a camera and put her plight on the airwaves, knowing that the public would not allow them to kill her.

Not wanting to have bad publicity, they renewed their efforts and finally sent her up to the Olympic Game Farm, which the Disney people had originally suggested. Disney had become involved in this facility as they wanted to have access to various animals for some of their movies. There my little bear became a movie star, joining other famous animals like Gentle Ben-- a huge brown bear-- Charlie the Lonesome Cougar, and other creatures including coyotes, badger, deer, and wolves. Over time the Game Farm became a well-known state attraction and now has lions, tigers, elk, bison, camels and many other animals too numerous to mention. One can drive through this huge facility and feed the animals out of the car window. I remember a big brown bear who would sit up and wave its huge paw in hopes of a slice of bread. One can buy a loaf of bread at the entry gate, so all the animals know that if one stops their car they might get a handout. When we eventually visited the Game Farm to see our bear, she stood up on her hind legs and put her front paws around Orville's waist, giving him a hug! It was good to know that the tiny little bear I rescued became a movie star. My Big Time Bear!

## 4: MEMORIES OF AUTUMN

### A Kiss of Rain

Even when one is alone for long periods of time, one need not dwell on self-pity. For several years, my husband was gone for six months at a time. One day in late August, an early fall rain persisted all morning. Gray clouds hung low. Tiring of my solitary housework, I paused to look out the window. The branches of the trees along the clearing waved in an ever-increasing breeze, but the clouds still clung to the mountains with stubborn resistance, like shining tight skin. Then came the wind with deft little fingers, and, peeling them from the hills, tossed them in the air to be carried away.

With the incoming sunshine I felt an urge to cancel any further house cleaning and wander through the freshly-washed woods. Our dog never refused an invitation to go walking, so away we went-- down the hill to the river, where grew a miniature rain forest consisting of huge maples, alders, and vine maples draped with moss.

The river murmured a bubbling conversation in answer to the blue jays and squirrels scolding my intrusion into their private world, while rain still dripped from the trees, creating music-- a soft melody of millions of drops. The noonday sun filtered down through the canopy, lending its brilliance to the green mosses and the leaves beginning to change into their fall colors. Around a bend in the trail, a low-hanging vine maple branch cushioned with moisture-soaked moss held, in suspension, a clear drop of rain. On a sudden impulse I touched my mouth to it, and allowed the cold sweet taste to slip between my lips. A kiss of rain.

## 'Twas a Dark and Stormy Night

The autumn wind was howling, whipping the branches of the trees into a frantic dance, and the rain rattled on the windows. When I went out to turn off the kitchen light to start getting ready for bed, I saw a little snow bird on the mat outside the glass sliding door. When it saw me, it hopped back and forth and pecked on the glass several times. I carefully slid the door open a bit and he hopped into the room. Looking around, he flew up onto the back of the kitchen chair. Then he spotted our large fish pond atrium, lined with different kinds of plants. That seemed like the perfect place for a small bird, and in he flew! Settling on the large stem of one of the plants, he settled in for the night, happy to be in safe from the terrible storm. When we got up the next morning, the storm had passed and the little bird was fluttering against the window wanting out. As soon as I slid the front door open, out he went-- the little bird that came in out of the storm!

## Cats and Rabbits

One afternoon, I went to see a neighbor to get some information from her. The back door by the carport was more convenient, and after knocking on it I stood waiting for an answer. Then a movement in the carport caught my attention. The neighbor's cat came strolling over. As he trotted up the steps to show off his fresh-caught prize, I saw a little bird's foot, frantically jerking back and forth, sticking out of his mouth! I reached down and gave the cat a spat on the head. Surprised, he dropped the bird, which flew away before he could react. That was one frustrated cat—and one lucky bird!

I once found a tiny baby wild rabbit, so small I could hold it in one hand. With a lot of care and bottle feeding it grew big enough to set free in the woods again.

## The Beauty of Autumn

Over a long lifetime, I have been privileged to see the Northern lights and several comets. The weather creates so many spectacular scenes with the wind and the clouds.

The wind is a creator. At times after a rain, a little breeze will start the quaking aspen's little golden leaves to clapping their hands, and the water drops clinging to the branches will flash brilliantly in rainbow colors as the sun strikes them. Then the breeze will shake the tree again, and the diamond drops will slip away.

There was a day that began with a soft gray kitten mist that gradually melted into rain. Another day, the warm autumn breeze wrapped soft arms around me, holding time still for a moment, then slipped away through the trees, rustling the leaves in passing.

Then one morning, the view out the window revealed a bright cold landscape; the frost had come, outlining every branch and twig on the trees. Below the house there were white meadows instead of green. The sun turned sparkling rainbow highlights on the frozen rain drops and on the gold autumn leaves, flashing signals to the day.

## The Frost Flowers

Winter brought all new wonders to our farm, with frost and icicles hanging from low branches over the creek. As I walked along its banks, I found a special group of weeds that the frost had created-- frost flowers, which only form under very cold conditions. The sun soon melted their fragile beauty, and I have only seen them once.

Morning sometimes presents oppressive elements of foreboding, as was the case for me not long ago. Mentally burdened, and feeling pressed by so many chores demanding my attention, I began to walk down to the barn to clean the stalls. The clear cold weather demanded my donning a warm hat, coat and gloves, while our pair of Lhasa Apso dogs danced and wagged in anticipation of a morning outing.

We usually take the dogs on long leashes, or they will go bounding off into the fields and woods in joyous pursuit of birds, deer, cows, or horses, completely oblivious to our calls to come back. They are such happy little creatures, and their company always brings me pleasure. As I walked down to the barn that morning, the beauty of the frost sparkling in the sun dazzled its way into the clutter of my mind, scattering my depressing thoughts asunder and replacing them with the joyous realization that this is my moment, and no one can ever take it from me!

After the barn chores, walking back to the house was pleasant in the warming sun. On the grass, frost turned liquid reflected rainbow colors, stimulating my dulled senses into motion. Who needs material riches of silver and gold when one can walk through a field of glittering diamonds such as this? For every winter snow there is a spring, for every sad song in the heart, the voice of hope will sing.

## 5: MAN'S BEST FRIEND

### All the Dogs of My Life

I think everyone should have a dog. They bring out the best in people—love, caring, and appreciation for the devotion they give so freely. From as far back as I can remember, I have always had one.

My first dog was a border collie mix that was in a pen at the dog catcher's. As soon as she saw my sister and I, she began to wag her stub of a tail and prance around by the fence, and she became our dog. Through the years Minnie took care of her girls, watching out for us. She did not approve of some of the things we did!

Once in a Lifetime

When we lived in Palouse, Washington, times were so different than they are now. Most people had an ice box for keeping food fresh, as refrigerators were a luxury. Our ice was delivered by a man driving a wooden horse-drawn wagon, which contained huge blocks of ice covered by a big canvas. He would chip off any size of ice block one needed to fit in their box. When he was finished, he would go on to his next customer, and that was our chance as kids to have some fun. We would run behind the wagon, catch hold of the back and hang on for as long as we could, swinging with the motion of the vehicle. Minnie would always follow, barking her disapproval. Minnie did not like cars either, and would rush at them, barking.

In those days, we were always getting into some kind of mischief, and by the weekend when our dad was home, we were often due for a spanking to alter our attitudes. Minnie was always there, trying to intervene on our behalf, barking and getting in the way of discipline. She was our constant companion.

A bit of history: When my father was a little boy living in Seattle, he remembered seeing the car traffic there. A few cars were silent, with no noisy motors, and he was told they ran on static electricity. Those cars soon disappeared from the streets and he found out that the inventor had sold the patent to a large auto manufacturer. It's taken a few generations for humanity to get those soundless electric vehicles back again!

At the beginning of World War II we moved near Bremerton, where the big Navy shipyard was. The owner of the small rental houses there had my dad manage these rentals, as well as run the small grocery store. One day a little fluffy female dog appeared at our back door, hungry and needing a home, and Minnie had a new friend!

The years slipped by, the store was sold, and our family moved onto a sailboat, the "Makua." This time Alaska was to be our destination, and we sailed through the Canadian waters of the Inside Passage all the way to Southeast Alaska.

The dogs did not care for boat life, but they enjoyed going ashore at various towns like Ketchikan, Wrangle, Juneau, Hoonah, and Skagway. Sitka was part of their life adventure, too. We overwintered in Ketchikan, but the hard sea life took its toll on Minnie. One day she slipped away, and was buried at sea in the boat harbor. Muffie took her place, and traveled back south with us to Washington, then on down the Pacific coast all the way to Newport Beach. That was great place for a small dog-- warm, sandy beaches to run on, and a big yard to play in!

Once in a Lifetime

Two years after Orville went into the Navy, we were married and rented a small house near San Diego, where he was stationed. Then we moved north, to Cardiff-by-the-Sea. We rented a little house that was built out of adobe. That was where we bought our little green conure parrot and named her "Seedie Moodie," as we could not have a dog there. Her story is told later on in this book.

One day we were surprised when a small dog with only three legs came to our door, needing a home and some loving care. We named him Bonzo, and he lived with us until Orville's ship left for Okinawa. Fortunately we had a friend who was stationed at a nearby Marine base who took him, so Bonzo joined the Marines! After two more years in the Navy, which included taking part in the first hydrogen bomb test in the South Pacific islands in 1954, Orville was finally discharged, and flew north to Pelican, Alaska, where I was helping my folks fish for salmon.

In the fall we rented a small house on the Kitsap Peninsula while we built our first home. Finally we could have our own dog, and we went to the Humane Society to find one. I always liked small, furry dogs, but the only one who came close was a curly dog that was part poodle and English sheepdog. We named her Mitzi and soon found out that no one had ever taught her a thing. She thought the rug in the house was the same as grass, and used it as her bathroom, and she never learned not to do it. She was so dumb, but we put up with her!

Just after we moved into our new house, we had an unusual little friend living under the back porch. Every evening it would come out to see if we had left a slice of bread for it, and it was so polite for a little skunk—it never used its spray defense until we got Mitzi, and she never learned not to chase it and receive her full spray in the face! Finally the skunk tired of the situation and moved away.

One spring, Orville bought a gillnet boat, and we sailed north to Alaska and Mitzi became a sea dog. Never smart, she was on the back deck one day and fell overboard! She did manage to swim, and we fished her out so she could be dumb another day. Her best times were when we would take our little skiff and row ashore to do some beachcombing. One time we hiked up to a little lake, and she really got excited when she saw a beaver swimming near the shore. She was always glad when the season ended and we went back to living on shore.

One day I had volunteered to help out the ladies' club sale downtown, and while I was there, a group of school children stopped in to see what was for sale. A little black-and-white shepherd-type dog followed them in, and when they left she stayed and lay down by me. She was really thin and weak. When it was time to go home and no one came to claim her, I took her to the veterinarian and found out she had distemper. With medication and loving care, she recovered, and Cindy was our new little dog!

One day, we found that Mitzi had gone to sleep in the nearby woods and had never woken up. At least we gave her a good life.

Cindy went on several trips to Alaska when we went commercial fishing, but her favorite place was our big yard surrounded by trees and a green lawn. One day, she found herself playing mother to a little baby black bear we'd found abandoned at a farm. That experience is narrated in 'Big Time Bear.'

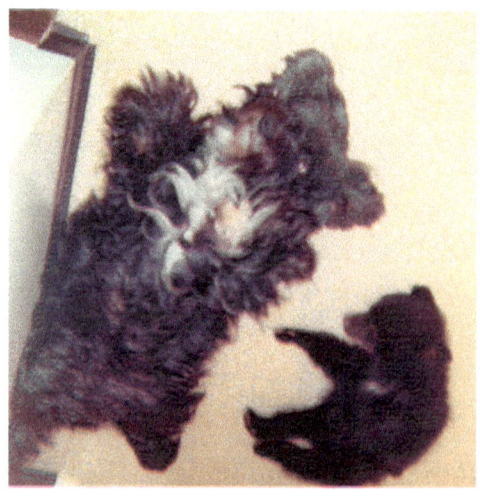

All of our dogs lived way past the average canine lifespan, as they were all loved and cared for. Cindy was a part-time sea dog and a part-time land dog. She also would ride in our airplane, and there again, would rather be at home in her yard!

It's always hard to lose a special pet. Photos and good memories help. My mother's little Lhasa Apso had puppies right after Cindy was gone, and we picked out a little golden male. He had dark fur around his eyes that made him look like a little owl. We named our new special puppy Scooter. Still a baby, he became a sea dog as we went North to fish on our new boat, the "Apollo."

Onboard, we had a little box lined with a soft blanket for him to sleep in. It was never used as Orville, who slept in the lower bunk, felt sorry for him when he whined and fussed at bedtime. He would lift him up and put him at the foot of his bunk. When he got up the next morning, Scooter would go up and nestle down on his pillow.

One day we anchored up in a little protected cove, and there on the beach was the full skeleton of a huge whale! We took two ribs and a back bone and still have them in our back yard , and here is a picture of Scooter on the biggest bone any dog has ever had!

I've always believed in talking to my pets, whether they're horses, dogs, or parrots, and Scooter got smarter the older he became. This picture shows how he liked to sit on the back of my chair and peek over my shoulder to beg for a snack!

Scooter always went everywhere with us, whether we were boating, driving, or flying. Camping and beachcombing were always great fun for him, seeing new places and scents.

After we lost our son, we moved to the Olympic Peninsula where we bought 110 acres. We built a new home there, and enjoyed being surrounded with fir, cedar and maple trees. There were three streams on our ranch and Scooter loved to wade in them on a hot summer day. There was some open pastureland there too, so eventually we started a small herd of beef cattle. The story of

Bruno the Bull is that of another animal I talked to, and also, of course, I talked to my horses.

Orville would spend his winters building and selling one or two houses, and then in the spring he would take the Apollo and spend the summer fishing, first for salmon, then tuna. That left me alone, except for little Scooter.

There was a time when my health failed, and I would spend my days lying close to the warmth of the woodstove, with Scooter nestled up close to me. He knew something was wrong, and stayed close to my side. When things finally improved, we would go for long walks down the road to the front driveway gate. One time we rounded a turn in the road and there was a black bear! Scooter ran after it, barking, and I ran after him, screaming for him to stop and come back! The bear panicked from all the noise we were making, and ran off into the deep woods. Scooter finally stopped, and I gathered up my precious dog for a hug and some loving.

I always want my special dogs to live forever, and when it doesn't happen, the loss is always painful. After Scooter was gone, we found another little Lhasa Apso, and of course, he became special like all the others. That breed comes from Tibet and were only let out of the country after the Second World War, as they were considered sacred temple dogs. Only pairs were allowed to leave the country. The breed soon became more well-known and we acquired the little golden puppy which we named Ping Shan Khan after looking up some Tibetan history. He was smart and cute in his ways; the only problem was that he didn't like the raccoons coming on the deck to eat the dog food we put out for them. He would run and jump against the glass sliding doors to try and scare them away. I would try to stop him, but he kept doing it.

One morning, he came down the hall dragging his hind legs and walking with his front paws only. I tried to get an appointment with our good vet, but the receptionists did not care about him and would not let me bring him in. So we went to another vet and she was so busy with a goat we had to wait for a long time, as the usual good vet was gone. When she finally came in, she she didn't know what to do with him. He was suffering, and we could not stand to let it go on, so he was put to sleep, no hope or help for him from that dumb vet.

My daughter then bought us a little Lhasa Apso puppy named Kham Ki Ling. He was full of energy and loved to play with his stuffed toys! When Christmas came around, we always wrapped some treats in gift paper for him, and he had great fun ripping them open to get the treats inside. He loved long walks to the creek, where it was great fun to play in the water. As usual, he became special to us, like all the other dogs we'd had. Going camping in our little travel trailer was his favorite thing to do, as there were always new places to explore, long sandy beaches, trails through the forests, or wading in the shallow water of the huge Columbia river. All of our dogs lived long lives with our love and care. It's always hard to lose one, but at least we have pictures, and the good memories they leave behind.

A long time passed before we began to think about another dog. Then a friend told us about a lady in a nearby town who raised Shih Tzus, so we went to see them. She lived in a mobile home and had a big fenced-in front yard. When we went in, we were surrounded with a huge family of little dogs. There were the mamma and papa of six puppies, and their aunt and uncle, all swarming around us like a swarm of bees!

I picked up several of the puppies and Orville picked up a fluffy little black and white male. The pup decided he was going to be our dog, and sat on Orville's lap while I looked at the others. Finally a cute, pug-nosed little brown and white female chose me—so we came home with two six-month-old babies!

We named the little female Buttons, because she had big brown eyes and a little button nose with a double row of front teeth—unusual for a dog. The little male we named Beaux, for 'boyfriend.' They go everywhere with us.

I talked to my dogs as I do with all animals, and they soon learned to understand people language. Beaux does his chores for treats and Buttons. He learned to get Orville his shoes or slippers, and to carry the little box that has the grooming brushes and combs in it. He also learned to pick up things I drop, carry out my bundle of recycled pastic shopping bags, and take in a little book from the front room when we go in to get ready for bed. He has favorite little stuffed toys that squeak, one of which he must have to take to bed with him at night.

Beaux and Buttons both seem to know when I'm having a bad day, and they come and sit with me in the recliner. In the morning when I come out to the front room, they are waiting to greet me by jumping in my lap for some loving. A few years ago I was sitting in the hall by the bathroom brushing out their coats as I do every day. When I was finished with Beaux, he went into the bathroom and began barking at the cabinet. I went to take a look and heard a crackling sound. When I opened the door, there were smoke and flames inside! Apparently the chimney lining had burnt out, leaving the cement blocks so hot it caught the wood behind the cabinet on fire! We had to call the fire department, as the flames had spread on up into the rafters in the ceiling. Orville tried to put it out by getting on the roof with the water hose and putting it down beside the chimney, but that did not work. It was the fire department who finally put it out. The water flooded the kitchen, and there was a lot of damage done. Beaux became our little dog hero, as he had warned us about the fire before it could spread to the whole house.

I brush our dogs every day, and take that time for a bit of loving. Beaux lays on my lap with his head on my chest, and I talk to him, letting him know how special he is. His hair has never been cut, and it is around eighteen inches long, touching the floor. Buttons always jumps up into the chair with me and lays close to my side until she gets too warm. When Beaux gets one of his stuffed toys and makes it start squeaking, Buttons comes over and begins to howl. That triggers Beaux and he howls back, and that starts a howl-in which goes back and forth!

My little dogs are still so precious to me, and they are my constant companions. As long as I live they will be with me. I remember hearing a quotation somewhere: "All dogs go to heaven." If so, I will find them all again sometime.

## Cat Tails

We never had a cat until we moved to a small cabin in the country while we built our present home. We then inherited several cats who lived in the barn near the cabin. One was white, and we called her Snow. The next kitten we named Agamemnon. The last was a beautiful black male who had white eyebrows, chest and four white paws. We called him Fonzie because he loved all his girls. He was what we called a Manx, because he did not have a tail, only a fuzzy fan of fur in place of one.

When we moved into our new house, the cats came with us. Agamemnon had kittens all like their daddy, with no tails. Then we went on a two-week trip and asked a relative to feed the cats while we were gone. When we came home all that was left of our kitties were several baby kittens, all dead from lack of food. The relative had not fed our adult cats either, and they too were all gone.

Later, we built a large barn to keep hay in for our new herd of cows. One day we looked up in the loft and there was a big grey cat. He was a stray who no one wanted because he was so ugly. He had pale yellow eyes and a flat, pushed-in face, one ear that was drooping down, and the other rather shredded, probably from being in fights. His new name was Cat Ugly. He lived in the barn for several years keeping the mouse population down. He was never friendly, maybe because he had had such a hard life in the past. We put a dish of food in the loft for him every day. Then, one day when we went to refill it, the old food was still there, and Cat Ugly was gone.

When the mice started taking over again, we decided to try to find another barn cat. Someone suggested we contact our local Animal Control. They had many kittens and house cats, several feral cats, and one that they said they were going to put down because he had bitten an elderly lady. We took him to save his life. They brought him over in a big cage and put it in the loft so he could get used to his new home. They said to let him out after a week, and they came back for the cage.

We kept a dish of food in the loft for him even though his main meals were the mice. Over time, he began to trust my husband, especially when autumn came and he had to get hay every day for the cows. Eventually this new cat let us pet him.

One morning while my husband was loading hay, he jumped into the cab of the truck and rode with him to the field where he fed the cows. From then on, it became a daily routine for him to supervise the feeding of the cows. When the hay had to be dropped to the ground from the upper loft, my husband used his excavator to lift the bales from the ground to the truck bed. Kitty had to supervise that operation too! He climbed onto the machine and sat on my husband's lap. When the hay was loaded, he would get into the truck cab to help feed the cows.

A name finally came to him—Smarty Cat! One day we took the pickup truck out to bring home the hay bailer from a job down the road. In jumped Smarty Cat, recognizing the chance for a fancy ride! Out the front gate and down the road we went to get the baler! After that, whenever we would go down to the barn he would hear the truck coming and be waiting to greet us and maybe catch another ride! We were lucky to have found Smarty Cat and to have had him for a friend.

## 6: WILDERNESS ADVENTURES

### Frogs and Ladybugs

As days turn into years, there is always another time to find beautiful or exciting things that occur in nature, and to anticipate what might be around the bend in the river of life.

When we lived in Medford, Oregon we went on many family outings, hiking up into the foothills above the town. We usually packed a picnic lunch and spent most of the day on our hikes. One warm day in early spring, we drove up to the end of Dead Indian Road, parked and walked up the hill. The new spring grass was just beginning to come up, and the warm sun brought out all the delightful scents of pine trees and buck brush. We noticed some bright color up ahead, and when we came closer saw a mass of brilliant red-orange lady bugs emerging from an old rotting tree stump. There were so many they made a little rustling sound as they crawled on the stump and the log alongside it. The warm sun signaled their mass movement soon to be scattered into flight by the soft breeze.

After we moved to western Washington, we would spend a week at a time in the summer camping near Horseshoe lake. When one is small, camping out in a tent is a big adventure. We went swimming every day and took long walks. One hot afternoon there was no wind. The quiet, cool woods beckoned and we went for a walk down an old logging road near the lake. Not far into the woods, we began to see tiny bright green tree frogs all hopping in the direction of the lake. We tried stepping gingerly around them, but the further we went the more frogs there were. Like the ladybugs, there were so many they became a mass, and we stood still watching, finally having to turn back because they covered the entire road in their undulating green movement to the lake.

Forest Sounds

In the early 50's I was fortunate enough to see Southeast Alaska before it was commercialized by tourism and tainted by greedy exploiters of its natural wonders. Traveling on our boat with my parents to buy fish, we made an overnight stop at the small Indian village of Hoonah. After having dinner and refueling our boat, I decided to go for a walk along the beach. I was feeling lonely and sorry for myself because my sister had married and I had no prospects of doing the same. Then a path leading into the woods distracted me from my worries.

The trail led into a different world, away from the sea and salt air. It was quiet and rather mysterious, with huge cedar and hemlock trees decorated with gray-green Spanish moss. The last of my sadness was dissipated by a little bird's song.

Suddenly there was a swish and rustle of wings as a huge raven settled on a broken snag near the trail. His feathers glistened black, with purple and blue-green highlights. Clicking his bill a few times, he cocked a bright eye in my direction, and I was transfixed as the bird began raven talk in soft tones. The Tlingit Indians fashioned many of the sounds of their language from the raven. Like crows, these birds only sing a delicate sweet song when they feel no human is present, screaming raucous calls when they are disturbed. Satisfied with his music, the raven took flight, leaving me with a sense of peace, and awareness of my surroundings. The sweet damp scent of moss, ferns and cedar filled the air. Shafts of warm sunlight sought entrance into this private world, lending brilliance to whatever it touched.

But what was that other sound? Where was it coming from? It certainly was not made by animals or humans! Listening intently, I followed the sunlight toward a minute popping-snapping sound, finally finding its source on a patch of emerald green moss. Kneeling down for a closer look, I saw that the moss had tiny stems with pinhead-sized bulbs on top. The warmth of the sun was causing the tiny capsules to burst with a snap-pop, releasing miniature puffs of pollen. Nature rewards infinite surprises of beauty and sound for those who only take the time to look and listen.

## Whales and Otters

The first time we went to Alaska, during the waning years of World War II, we sailed on our 32-foot sloop rig sail boat, the "Makua." Built in a Seattle boat yard and designed by Ed Monk, it had a six foot keel, thick four-inch cabin construction and heavy Port Orford cedar planking. Built for foul weather, it emitted a feeling of safety, but with its small engine and limited fuel capacity, we sailed whenever the winds favored it.

Sailing north in the protected Inside Passage, we left the Queen Charlotte Sound to be suddenly surrounded by a large pod of whales. Making their way up the channel alongside us, they rolled to the surface to blow puffs of spray, then ducked back under the water, only to surface again in a few minutes. I was standing by the side rail holding onto the stay when one curious whale rose right alongside the boat. Matching the speed of the vessel, it rolled to one side, and I could see its eye looking at us. It rolled back, and its blow hole emitted a huge spout of water and air-- really bad air, smelling of half digested fish. A ton of mints would not have cured its bad breath! Then, as quickly as they had appeared, the pod waved a farewell, with their great tails slipping at last under the water.

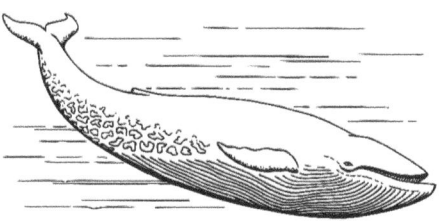

While we were commercial salmon fishing in southeast Alaska, there were generally whales present, and once we saw a huge one jump completely out of the water. It seemed to hang for a moment in the air before plunging back into the sea with a massive splash. Once while we were trolling, a whale shark swam between the tag lines and the hull of the boat. Its head was over three feet wide. It was gray-brown, with large darker spots on its back. Somehow it did not tangle in the lines or touch the boat, but we were grateful when it swam on past the bow and off on its own pursuits.

Dolphins escorted many of our passages, dashing back and forth by the bow of the boat, at times coming close to touching the hull. They seem to be playing a game of tag, breaking the surface of the water with puffs of air from their blow holes, then diving down again deep into the green depths only to shoot back up, seeming to dare the boat to catch them.

Eagles were ever present along the shore, roosting in the tall firs or sailing out over the water looking for fish to catch on the fly. Once we saw something struggling in the water about a hundred feet from shore. As we drew close, we could see a huge eagle in the water, headed for the beach, using its wings like oars. Apparently it had sunk its claws into a salmon too large to lift. Once an eagle's talons are dug into its prey, it is difficult for them to release it until they land. Fortunately, this bird was close enough to shore that eventually it would reach safety, and the reward of a hearty meal.

We had a small skiff lashed to the deck of our boat, and when we anchored at the end of the day's run, down went the skiff into the water, and we would row ashore to go beach combing, walking and exploring. There are so many isolated islands, bays and little sheltered coves in Alaska, there is always something new to see.

Having anchored in a small bay on Dundas Island south of Ketchikan, we were rowing our skiff alongside a rocky shoreline when we were surprised by what looked like a huge sea serpent with a long brown body. It was undulating in and out of the water, and looked to be about ten feet long. It headed for the beach, and our sea monster turned out to be three large sea otters, following one after another! They came out of the water, each almost upon the tail of the other, and dashed up into the woods.

## Brown Bears in Alaska

The coast of southeast Alaska is a labyrinth of large and small islands, with passages one can easily get lost in without a chart. Once we were running alongside a small island, with another larger one about five miles off in the distance, when we saw something swimming in the water heading for the beach. We slowed the boat to watch, and to find out what it was. Field glasses revealed it was a huge brown bear! We had a movie camera, and Dad went up on the front deck to film it. I had an old still camera that I pulled out of the case, but it had to be focused. I was standing with the sliding door of the cabin open, trying to find the animal in the view finder-- an extremely dumb thing to do. I had heard of a big seine boat, the crew of which tried to do the same thing-- take pictures of a bear-- and that bear had climbed onto the boat and proceeded to send one of the crew up the mast, and the others into the cabin and over the side. The bear had taken the deck of that boat apart!

Meanwhile, this bear kept swimming towards our boat. I managed to snap two pictures, but when I looked up, it was within a few feet of our vessel, which had slowed to a near stop. Huffing and puffing, it reached out with a huge paw to catch hold of the old car tire we had hanging as a fender from the rail. Horrified, I watched the tire turn from round to oblong with the weight of the bear, which now had one front paw on the tire and was clawing at the hull with the other, trying to climb up onto the boat. I slammed the cabin door shut and put the boat in gear. The bear's grasp on the tire was torn loose by the sudden surge and the creature's own massive weight. It tried to catch hold of the boat again, leaving huge, deep claw marks in the wooden planks. Then we watched, amazed, as it swam to the stern and thence on toward the beach. When it reached the shore, the huge animal ran up the steep bank and into the woods. We were awed to see that after such a long swim, the bear could still run so fast.

Around Juneau there were miners who hired watchmen to look after their buildings, preventing people from helping themselves to artifacts and from trying to go into the mines. We met one watchman who had an old truck which he used to ride up a hill on a narrow road to check on a mine. It was a lonely job, and after visiting with him for awhile, he offered to take us up to see the mine. Mom and Dad rode inside the cab, while my sister and I stood up in the bed, holding onto the bar in back of the cab. Suddenly a huge brown bear came out onto the road ahead of us and started running up the hill. The watchman said, "Hold on, and we'll see how fast he can run!" The old truck roared up the hill, the bear staying ahead of it. The speedometer clocked 40 mph, but the bear was still winning the race! The animal finally turned off the side of the road and disappeared into the thick woods. This was proof to me that one should never run from an angry bear-- the bear will win the race every time.

## Sledding in Juneau

Years ago while we were living in Juneau, Alaska, fortune brought me an invitation to join a group of young people on a bobsled ride out to the Mendenhall Glacier Lodge near the lake. The long sled held around ten people in a seated position, packed front to back, each one holding to the person in front. The sled started off with a jerk amid screams of excitement and laughter, pulled by a chained-up flatbed truck. As we picked up speed, the air was filled with fine crystals of snow swirling up from behind the truck. It stung our faces, increasing the thrill. With the moon behind us, the clear night sky was filled with stars made brilliant by the freezing weather. Racing along over the icy road, we were soon out of town and into the country. Trees laden with snow sped by, and hills and banks of snow and ice glistened and sparkled as dramatic shadows among the trees enhanced the scene.

Others of our group had gone ahead to build a fire, so upon arriving at the lodge everyone was ready to go in by the big fireplace filled with logs, which made a crackling invitation to gather close and warm up. Someone brought hot cocoa and other spirits for anyone who wished it. One could look out the windows across the smooth, snow-covered, frozen lake to the glacier, which seemed to give off a pale blue-green aura. We sang songs, and told jokes and stories.

Then, all too soon, it was time to start back. With the moon gone, the black sky made the stars brighter than before, infinite space never-ending, with the milky way and far galaxies visible. As everyone was gathering outside near the sled, the Northern Lights appeared over the mountains, delaying our departure-- sheer, pale, undulating curtains of light, continually changing form, adding pale greens or pinks, then melting away again.

The cold finally urged us to squeeze onto the sled and start homeward. The return ride was as exciting as before. Then the lights of town announced the beginning of a fantastic memory.

## Life Savers

When my father was a boy living in Seattle, he once saved a little girl's life; and when Orville was young, he saved two little boys from drowning in Twin Lakes. It must run in the family, because I once saved a little girl from drowning too!

The Alaskan fishing season had ended, and we ran south with a fisherman friend. A long day's run ended in Friday Harbor. After dinner, my folks went aboard our friend's boat, the "Tacora," while I remained on our boat to play the piano. Engrossed in Chopin, I became dimly aware of their little four-year-old girl playing on the stern of their boat.

Once in a Lifetime

Suddenly I heard a huge splash! I hit the back doors of the cabin and rushed onto the cockpit of our boat. Looking down into the water, I spotted the little girl floating about six inches under the surface. Her eyes were wide open, her hair was fanned out from her head, and her hands and arms extended from her sides. The splash had turned into glass; it appeared as though she was looking up through a window.

Not one to get my feathers wet, I hung onto the side of our boat and reached down to the water. She reacted by reaching up to me, and I pulled her out of the water. Fortunately she had not breathed any and came onto the deck dripping and crying. The grownups heard what was going on, and rushed on deck. I am forever grateful to have had the ability to solve this crisis, and to be able to see and solve, with quick thinking, the problems I've encountered.

Barbara Fisk

## To Touch Eternity

August 1993 found my husband and I flying to Alaska in our Cessna 182. Fortune was ours, as it was the most unusual clear, warm weather the local residents had ever witnessed.

Alaskan glaciers are living witnesses to the beginning of time. Flowing from immense ice fields high above the waterways, grinding their way down the mountains in a backward rotation from under to top, some advance, while others, melting, retreat. Others end up in the labyrinth of waterways in Southeast Alaska. It is hazardous to approach too close in a boat, as many glaciers dig beneath the floor of a bay. As they begin to melt, huge icebergs break off the floe, bursting up out of the water like a rocket launched from a submarine. It is also unwise to approach too close to icebergs of size in a boat. Glacial ice is two-and-a-half times denser than man-made ice, which causes seven-eighths of any iceberg to remain under the water. As the water laps at its sides and melts underneath, the ice can become top heavy. There have been many boats sunk by a berg rolling over and shattering the hull, or lifting it out of the water.

The face of a glacier is constantly sluffing away, huge chunks letting go and crashing into the water, creating miniature tidal waves. Varying hues of intense cobalt blue are revealed. Glaciers carry along rocks and debris, leaving long, curving, dirty trails of varying widths behind as they advance. When the ice flows along the rocky sides of a mountain, the ice smooths it like a knife frosting a cake. Receding ice flows leave behind mounds of gravel, boulders, sand and silt, creating gray-green ponds and lakes. Huge deep valleys are left behind, with the ribbons of creeks and rivers slicing through lush green grassy meadows and willow-lined marshes.

When flying over the coastal glaciers, we found many had receded at an alarming rate. Some which had crowded the headwaters of bays we had been into thirty to forty years before had vanished, leaving huge, scooped-out trenches. Others, cut off from the ice fields, were gray and dead in appearance. Flying over the active flows, one could look down into the crevasses between the jagged, saw-toothed clusters of ice. On another day we flew Glacier Bay, starting where the ice enters the water, then flying up the floe as one would drive a steep winding mountain road. Our airspeed slowly dropped as we climbed. There was a breathtaking panorama at the top. Ice fields covered the whole horizon like the unending steppes of Russia, with only the very peaks of the mountains breaking through the glistening snow. The thought occurred to me that this was not the place to have an engine failure, and it was certainly not the place to camp out in a tent as some people we saw, who had been flown onto the glacier by helicopter.

On our homeward flight, we landed at Juneau. The airport there was built on the flats created by the Mendenhall Glacier. In times past, before the airport sprawled out over the land, lagoon berries grew in abundance there. Now their bright red, unusually flavored goodness was smothered with blacktop. The Mendenhall Glacier is slowly receding, leaving behind a huge gray-green colored lake afloat with icebergs. Many years ago, this ice was harvested by an enterprising person who picked up the ice by boat, then trucked it to town and sold it to the restaurants and bars. Glacial ice melts more slowly than regular ice, thus it does not water down drinks.

We stood on the shore of the lake, listening to the cracks, creaks and groans, as it is a living glacier. The winds sweeping down from the ice fields carried an indescribable scent, sweet and cold, of eons past. Walking along the shore, I picked up a piece of ancient, crystal clear, smooth ice. The clean blue sky, the whisper of the wind in the willow trees, the feel of the ice... I felt I had touched the fringes of eternity.

Barbara Fisk

## 7: BY LAND, SEA AND AIR

### The Runaway

Horses. I have been fascinated by them since I was a child. My greatest desire was to have one of my own. Only on rare occasions was I afforded the opportunity to ride one, and consequently I never learned to ride well.

The first pony ride I had ended in disaster. The pony took off down the field at a gallop, I bounced once on his back, then his rump, and then lit on the ground. Still, whenever a carnival came to town that had a pony ride, I always wanted one, even if the ponies were in a pen, going around in a circle.

It took the passing of many years before I finally bought my own horse. Even after I was grown and married with two children, the desire was always there. Finally my lifelong dream came true with the purchase of a six month old colt. The children named him Sun Dance. He was a strawberry roan with a white mane and tail. Because of his coloring, in the old cowboy days he would have been called a "Sunday horse." They always rode their best-looking horses to town.

It would almost two years before I could ride him, so while he was being trained by a friend, I bought an older horse from an old-time cowboy who taught me a lot about them.

My cowboy friend had equipment for packing into the high backcountry. He taught me how to put it on a horse and tie it down with a diamond hitch. Now things have changed and few, if any, know how to tie that diamond hitch. We packed into the Olympic mountains as well as the Cascades, and saw a lot of unusual things. We witnessed a large herd of elk crossing a valley, and a big black bear that ran as fast as he could to get away from our horses and noise. We enjoyed the quiet beauty of the wilderness, the scent of wildflowers and fir trees, and the sight of squirrels, birds and marmots peeking out from behind the big boulders along the trail. All of these are memories that still return to me in the quiet of night, or when I am at rest alone in the daytime.

Back at home, our accommodations for my horses was limited, but a kind neighbor allowed me to picket the horses in her large unfenced field alongside the highway near town. I would walk them down the hill in the morning to graze and bring them home in late afternoon.

One day my husband Orville came home early and went with me to lead the horses. After taking the long picket line off the halter of Peanuts, the big black gelding, he suggested I ride that horse and he would lead Sun Dance. Fashioning a makeshift rein out of the lead rope and fastening it to the gelding's halter, he helped me up onto the horse's back and then went to get the yearling.

Inexperienced at riding bareback, I felt uneasy. The horse sensed my apprehension and began to trot. All my efforts to stop him failed. When he reached the end of the gravel drive, I tried pulling his head around to turn him back into the field and only succeeded in heading him down the hill. Fifty feet ahead was the intersection of a busy two-lane highway. Cars and seconds zipped by as the trot turned to a canter and we headed into the intersection. Stopped on the opposite side of the road was a car filled with teenage boys. To them the scene must have appeared comical, prompting them to wave and yell, "Ride 'em cowboy!"

Startled, the gelding turned and headed down the center line of the main highway at full gallop. His shoes struck the blacktop pavement with skidding sounds. If he or I fell! Images of broken bones and ground flesh came into my mind. I was aware of the look of consternation and disbelief on my husband's face as we flew by. There was no knight in shining armor on a white steed, or any good guy in a white hat to rescue me from impending disaster!

The downhill slope of the highway ahead obscured the oncoming traffic. There was no time to allow my life to pass in review. I had to stop the horse some way! *Peanuts, what a stupid name for a big black horse,* nonsense, more seconds, *think!* I could hear the swishing sounds of air rushing in and out of the horse's nostrils.

*Think!* Wind rushing in my face, heart wildly thumping, more seconds, there must be a way, *think!* Suddenly my memory flashed back ten years to an article I had read in Reader's Digest about a girl with a runaway horse, and how she had saved her own life. This was the only chance I had.

Peanuts was part draft horse, with a thick, strong neck which would surely support my one hundred and three pounds. Gripping his shoulders with my knees, leaning forward to partly lay on his neck and reaching out, I placed my hands over his eyes, then took them off. I knew if he came to a sudden halt he could slip and fall, or I could go flying off over his head and grind into a little ball of grease on the pavement. I kept repeating hands-on, hands-off his eyes until he began to slow down, then finally stopped. Grasping a handful of his thick mane I slid down from his back to the pavement and led the horse to the side of the road only moments before a large semi truck-and-trailer topped the rise and roared past, followed by a string of eight or ten cars.

Walking back toward home with trembling knees of jelly, I heard myself whispering, "Thank you, God, thank you!" Then came a flood of gratitude to the girl who had previously shared her experience, and to Readers Digest for printing it. I truly believe I would not be alive today if it were not for that article etched in my memory, lying dormant for so many years, then returning to meet my need of the moment.

One of my favorite horses was a beautiful Arabian. He would run across the field with his head high and his tail floating like a flag behind him. But eventually the passage of years indicated my time with horses was over. I recognized this when I had a problem lifting my saddle up on a horse's back, and had to climb up on a box to mount. Still, all that fun and adventure is tucked away in my memory, to be enjoyed again whenever I wish.

## The Watchful Sea

The sea is not always the romantic place portrayed in so much literature. It is ever watchful with green greedy eyes, waiting for the careless and foolhardy to slip or make a mistake, and the sea takes them down forever. When we sailed down the west coast from Washington to California the sea did not treat us with kindness.

It was fairly good sailing for the first few days. We took turns on the night watch, my Dad and I until midnight, my sister and mother the rest of the night until around six A.M. We had just exchanged watches. 1 was beginning to take off my warm cloths, and my sister was just climbing out into the cockpit when Mom shouted,

"We're on the beach!" A huge wave broke completely over the boat, and the only reason they were not washed overboard was because my sister was holding on the boom rope and mother to the tiller.

Dad and I rushed up on deck and sent them below. As another wave approached, we turned the boat into it. Dad tried to start the engine and it failed. While I held the tiller he went below, opened the engine room door, and a flood of water rushed out. After several more attempts, the engine started.

We kept heading off shore. The sea around us shone iridescent with phosphorus from the churning and breaking of the waves. The big jib had torn loose from the traveling block and the turnbuckle was whipping back and forth, ripping the sail. I worked my way forward and caught hold of the sail while Dad lowered it, and we lashed it to the deck. We set the storm sail, lashed the tiller and went below to assess the damage and put on dry clothes. The violent force of that first wave had loosened one of the glass shades on the gimbaled oil lamp and thrown it against the cabin wall so hard that it stuck there until we pried the shattered pieces out. The only way for us to get warm was to get into our bunks for the rest of the night.

The next day, we used the direction finder and found we had not been on the beach, but had gone across a group of five-fathom shoals. We headed to Goose Bay, Oregon, one of the few accessible bays to anchor in along the coast, to dry out and get the sail mended. When we reached the breakwater, the engine would not start. The wind had dropped and we had no way to proceed, with the beach on one side and the huge rocks of the breakwater on the other. Dad fired off his Very pistol with a distress flare, and fortunately it was sighted. The coast guard came and towed us in. One of the sailors said it was a good thing we arrived when we did, as in a half hour more the bar would have been breaking and we could not have made it. Our little dog was most grateful to be able to go to the beach, instead of in the cockpit.

Arrival at San Francisco

After a month the engine was back in working order, the sail mended, and we headed on down the coast. The third day out, the wind began to pick up again. In a matter of hours it was howling, and the seas surged to an unbelievable height. We put on the storm sail and found with only that little sail we were still logging nine knots, while the hull design of the "Makua" was six knots! A huge wave would build up behind the boat, ready to break, then pass under and away, letting the boat slide down the back side only to rise again on the next one. We found out later that the storm had gale force winds of one hundred miles an hour with fifty foot waves!

We kept track of our position off the coast with the direction finder, and when we were off San Francisco we headed in shore. The storm had blown itself out, and fog greeted us as we neared the bay. We began to see tidal trash and sea birds. The only sounds were the gulls, the bell on a big red buoy ringing, and the water murmuring past the hull. Suddenly a beautiful big sailboat came slipping out of the fog. It was the boat which carried the pilots for the big ships coming into San Francisco bay, and we hailed it. We had no idea where to go in the huge bay, and took on one of the pilots to guide us in. He said it was a first for him, as we were the smallest vessel he had ever piloted.

The Golden Gate bridge was true to its name. It was so foggy. All we could see was the golden glow of the lights on the bridge as we motored under it and entered the bay. A very tired and grateful crew of four docked in Sausalito Bay opposite the prison island, Alcatraz.

We lingered there for several weeks, as my Dad found an old school friend he had known when living in Hawaii. We also found he had a cousin who had a ranch in the foothills above the bay. They invited us to visit and go riding their horses. On one of our rides we went up to the ruins of author Jack London's house. It had burned, leaving a huge stone fireplace, chimney and foundation still standing. On another ride, we were crossing a huge field when the big gelding I was on decided to go for a run with the dumb novice on his back. All my *whoa-ing* and pulling on the reins did no good. He finally stopped when the trees and brush barred his way at the end of a short road. I had surprised myself, my uncle and sister as I had managed to stay on by clinging to the saddle horn.

A special treat was going to the huge art museum in San Francisco. There was one painting that is still vividly etched in my memory. It was a young child holding a rose with a single drop of dew on a red petal. It looked so real, as though it could fall off at any second. The colors were so alive in the clothing, face and hair. Someday I want to go back and see if it is still there, and renew a beautiful memory.

## Seedie Moody

My husand and I were married while he was still in the Navy, so we moved a lot. We had a little rental house north of San Diego, and could not have a dog. One time when we went shopping, we saw a little parrot in the window of a pet shop. When we went in, the little bright green head topped with red and blue feathers bobbed up and down, like it was telling us it needed a home. We had found a pet who could travel and move with us!

We named her Seedie Moody, as there were times when she let her temper show, and other times when she would sit peaceably on a hand or shoulder. In time, she slowly began to pick up words from us as no one had bothered to teach her at the pet shop. I was always laughing at her antics, and as time passed the sound of my laughter was included in her vocabulary.

Orville made a little playpen out of wood, with a ladder to climb up to a perch, and also a swing and a tiny bell she would tap with her beak to make it ring. When it was safe, we would let her spend most of the day in it, and even have lunch with a small dish of sunflower seeds on a tray.

When we found out Orville's ship was going to leave on Sea Trials and be gone for several months, I decided to pack up our few possessions, rent a little U-Haul trailer and head north to help my folks go fishing in Alaska. Seedie became a traveling bird, sitting on top of the things in the over-packed car.

The boat was very livable, with two bunks in the bow and a small toilet. The main cabin or wheelhouse was spacious, with a long bench toward the back. The wheel and compass on the left allowed space for Seedie's playpen, while the after-cabin held the stove, sink, and cupboards for the galley. A large table and benches graced one side, while a piano was bolted to the bulkhead on the other. The area left in the stern held the fishing gear and side boxes to put the fish in.

Heading north through the Inside Passage was an adventure. At times the water was rough, but other days were flat calm. When it was nice, Seedie would get to stay on her playpen which we put on the flat space near the window in the pilot house. Her cage was anchored down in the flat space in the back. There was a chart table attached to the ceiling on hinges, so it could be let down to view the sea charts. It was held at an angle with a heavy string on each side. When it was closed, the strings would hang down in a loop. Seedie would climb up and get hold of it, causing it to slide down. She would scream and laugh on the short ride, then go back and do it again.

The small harbor where we sold our salmon had limited space at the floats. One day there was no space left, so we tied up to another boat at the dock. Seedy soon was out of her cage and onto the playpen near the window. I was sitting on the bench with my camera about to take a picture of her, when a large cat jumped onto the deck from the boat next to us. When it saw Seedie, it jumped on the window in an effort to catch a free meal. I shooed the cat away and we made sure we did not tie up to that boat again.

During the fishing season, Orville was discharged from the Navy and flew up to Pelican where there was a small village and fish cannery. The summer slipped by, and when the season ended we headed south before the fall storms arrived. We bought an acre of wooded land and built our own house. Seedie went back to being a land bird. Her play stand was put near a big window where she could see the front yard and tall trees. This was much better than green water, and bouncing around in her cage when the sea was rough. Seedie remained our special pet for many years.

## Running Wild

Early in the morning of July 1980, the phone rang in my bedroom, waking me up with a start when I had intended to be lazy and sleep in. It was Orville, my husband, so that made it all right. He said, "Honey, we just came in from a tuna trip and Ken and Dee want to spend a few days here in Eureka. Why don't you fly down and join us?"

I was wide awake by now and answered, "Great idea! I'll bring some fresh fruit, meat and the cookies I baked yesterday! Before I leave, I can call the FAA and check the weather en route. What is it like down there?"

He replied, "There are a few clouds, but the sun is out, and it's supposed to be a nice weekend."

I did a quick mental calculation of how long it would take to get ready and said, "I should be able to take off by ten thirty. I topped off the fuel tanks after my last flight, and it should probably take about four and a half hours of flight, so I should be there around two thirty."

I was excited about flying our Cessna 182 and the thought of spending time with Orville. He was a commercial fisherman and gone six months out of the year, so any time we could spend together was precious. I hurried with dressing and quick breakfast, packed clothes for the weekend and our little dog Scooter's food and bedding. Scooter did not care much for flying although he would do anything to be with his family. After fastening him to the seat belt by his leash and loading everything else in the baggage compartment, hauling the heavy airplane out of the hangar took all the strength I had left. There were times when it was frustrating to be only five foot two and weighing only one hundred and three pounds!

It took time to do the usual pre-flight checks of oil, draining the gas lines to check for water and pulling the propeller through several turns to move the oil around in the engine. I checked the door, fastened the seat belt and laid out the charts, pilot guide and navigation instruments necessary for flying. Master switch on, the gyros made their winding-up noises and I turned on the fuel. I pulled the fuel injector twice, adjusted the throttle and finally turned the ignition key. The prop turned over several times and the engine fired and roared into action. I ran it up to 1750 RPM, checked right and left mags and the carburetor head. Air suction OK, oil pressure, engine head, check mags again. Then I adjusted trim, checked the ailerons and taxied into takeoff position. I looked at the compass and set the altimeter, double-checked the ground elevation on the instrument panel and saw everything was right. Releasing the foot brakes, I pushed myself back into the seat, roaring down the runway at sixty, then seventy MPH, and finally lifted off, released from the earth and all its daily chores and cares.

After adjusting the prop and engine speed, I set a climb for five thousand feet and laid out the charts on the passenger seat to work out a course for Eureka, which is on the northern California coast. Pilots usually make a check list of radio frequencies near large airport control zones, flight advisory stations, and VOR, necessary for a cross-country flight, but this time I relied on my experience and did not take the time to file a flight plan-- breaking a flight safety rule. The weather was good and time passed rapidly, with constant cross-checks from two VORs which showed my exact position on the chart. I was using visual references such as towns, railroads, highways and rivers to verify my progress.

Between navigation checks, I relaxed and let my mind drift, looking forward to the weekend with Orville. I thought about our beautiful son, why God had taken him from us when he was only fourteen. Tears slipped down my cheeks. No, I could not think about that now and let it interfere with my flying. Blinking the tears away and blowing my nose, I glanced into the mirror fastened to the sun visor. I did not want to arrive at Eureka with a big red nose and red-rimmed eyes. After checking my makeup and brushing my hair, I glanced at my watch. By now I should have been close to Eureka.

The scattered clouds below had gathered together, and the high stratus was dropping down ahead, forming a wedge at the center which was an ominous dark gray. The flight had taken longer than I had calculated, and there was only fifteen minutes of fuel left in the tanks! The gauges flapped back and forth with every movement of the plane. I was not licensed for IFR flying, although in my flight training I had spent several hours with my instructor using a hood to obscure outside references and flying on instruments only. Still, I was not about to fly into that black abyss, and searching for an alternative I saw a hole in the overcast which revealed the sun shining on a bright sandy beach with the ocean waves breaking on it. A sucker hole, as pilots call it! Just what was needed! Never one to panic in an emergency, always thinking my way through, I made a sharp turn and descended at the same time, dropping down through the clouds, and came out of them over the water, with enough clearance to fly between them and the beach.

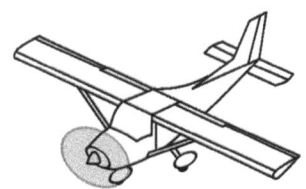

By now the fuel gauge needles had stopped flopping, indicating there was not enough fuel left to slosh around in the tanks. Then another problem surfaced-- I was coming under a heavy rain storm, which blinded my forward vision. Using the beach on the left and the water beneath as references, I kept on until I cleared the rain shower. Time was running out when I spotted an aircraft flying to my far left. The airport had to be just ahead!

I frantically searched the chart to find the radio tower frequency, thinking I should have this all down pat with a flight plan next time. There it was! "Eureka tower, this is Cessna N3117 Yankee. I would like airport advisory."

Landing safely, I was relieved to be back on the ground, and I had a feeling of pride and self-confidence when I spotted Orville coming from the terminal. He was proud of his wife and hurried out to give me a big hug and kiss, saying, "You did another of your great three-point landings!"

After tying down the plane, unloading baggage and lifting Scooter to the ground, he promptly sprinkled the airplane tire, showing his contempt for the noisy machine!

It was always a pleasure to see the look on peoples' faces when they realized a little red-headed lady was the pilot of the aircraft that had just landed, but my bubble of self-esteem was burst when I was called to the phone by an air traffic controller from the larger airport to the north of the one in Eureka. His voice expressed disapproval as he asked for an explanation of why I had violated airspace, forcing an approaching aircraft to abort its landing! I ate crow and humble pie, and explained that the airport had been obscured by the heavy shower and I didn't know I was in controlled airspace and did not have time to call and advise him. He said, "Do you realize I could pull your license?" I ate more humble pie, apologized, and managed to talk my way out of a serious violation.

This bad experience faded quickly as we had a wonderful romantic weekend, dinner out, and long sightseeing trips up and down the coast. We stopped at various tourist traps and drove through the redwoods with our friends. All who read about the redwood forests should go see them-- giants that grow to the sky, with moss and green ferns below.

Time melted away, and all too soon our friends were saying goodbye. It was time to fly home as the tuna awaited in the Pacific ocean. Orville hugged and kissed me, saying, "Be careful, and call me when you get home!"

So, with a good weather report and a flight plan filed, Scooter and I took off for home. The sun shone through broken clouds two thousand feet above the airfield as I made a circling climb. Looking back, I could see miniature people scurrying around like ants, and the cars on the road resembled little beetles. Deciding not to fly below the broken clouds, I headed upward towards the pale sun.

Suddenly it disappeared behind a thick white mass, with no visibility or references available. There was a feeling of being pressed back in my seat, then the pull of G's as the airplane began to run wild, out of control. The indicator dials spun, first showing the airplane was headed straight down! Frantically I pulled back on the yoke and the dials spun in reverse, indicating a thirty degree climb. With my heart thumping and my breath coming in jerks, I realized I had vertigo. *The instruments, stupid! Look at the instruments! You could go into a tailspin and not recover-- crash!*

*Forget what's outside. Believe your instruments,* my flight instructor had said. Checking them for climb and descent, then the wings for level and setting a five degree climb rate, it was only moments until the sun appeared again, and breaking out on top of the clouds, the blue sky beckoned. Was it my Irish luck, and my quick mind that had brought me out of two dangerous situations on this trip? Or was it something in Psalm 91, near the end where it says, "He shall give his angels charge over thee, lest thou dash thy foot against a stone." Saying a little prayer of thanks, I set the course for home.

It was more than five years after this experience before I could overcome my mental block and use the word "vertigo" to describe what had taken place.

# AFTERWORD

## "The Garden of the Mind"

Fortune has given us the opportunity to live in the country, where we are surrounded by the beauty of living, growing things, but for those less fortunate who must dwell in the cities, there are beautiful flowers of a different kind. Bright faces of children; the performing arts; and above all, music. There are galleries, museums, and stores filled with an infinite variety of fascinating items.

Regardless of where you may live, be sure to enjoy all good which comes your way. Allow no one to burst your bright balloon of life. Tend carefully your garden of the mind, lest weeds of stress, gossip, hate, and unkind remarks overgrow that which is precious. Reap the plentiful harvest of moments, for if you seek, you will find something good in the promise of each new day. If possible, share those moments with someone.

Since I came into this world in 1929, this country has changed dramatically. There is so much bad news on the TV, in the newspapers, and there is so much political turmoil it is difficult to find even a few good reports. Morals are being lost, and the public education system is not teaching the most important things about our country's history.

I was recently lamenting the fact that there was so much turmoil and bad news in our country. It seemed like it was going downhill fast, along with the human race. Then my faith was renewed by two small acts of kindness.

Because of Orville's disability, we are allowed to shop in the store on the big military base in our area. We had bought a new microwave oven, and Orville was trying to move it from the shopping cart to the back seat of the car. A young boy came and offered to help. The task accomplished, I thanked him and praised his good manners. It was such a pleasure to meet a teenager who cared for others when one sees so many on TV and the streets and parking places that don't seem to care for anything but tapping their cell phones with their thumbs.

The second pleasure which we encountered happened at the same military base. We were waiting in line at a sandwich shop. The man in front of us started to talk to Orville when he saw his cap, which said "Lifetime Member VFW." When his order was completed and he saw that ours was also, he asked if we wanted a soda drink. Orville said, "Root beer!" The stranger paid for his own meal and, turning, smiled and said, "Your order is already paid for." Such a nice gesture from a complete stranger!

My grandmother traveled west with her family in a covered wagon. Along the way, they found a man lying under a shade tree by the side of the road. He had been scalped by Indians and left for dead. Somehow he had survived, and they took him to be cared for at the next town they came to.

Afterwards, when the wagon train came to a big fort in Arizona, they saw Geronimo chained to a post on display outside the front gate. According to the history books and the westerns on TV, he was treated fairly—but chained to a post? I don't think so. The textbooks aren't always accurate.

As if faulty history isn't enough, the public education system is also failing to teach our students enough standard math and science. Texting others instead of having personal contact with them has become the norm. Too many people are living their lives in those little plastic boxes which flash constantly changing images to distract their attention, removing their senses from the beauty of the world all around them.

This country was founded on the Christian religion and values, but one has to look hard now to find those who care about others in need. My daughter Cheryl once said, "If everyone would help just one person in need, the world would be a better place." This is part of my reason for writing "Once in a Lifetime--" as a reminder that there is beauty and good in the world to look for and find.

I never thought I would open the gate to the secret garden of my memories, because of those who had trampled the beautiful flowers and left hurt behind; but I have finally done so with the hope that this book will bring pleasure to those who read it.

Now, with a soft sigh, the garden gate swings closed. I will leave you with this Biblical verse:

"Finally, brethren,
Whatsoever things are true
Whatsoever things are honest
Whatsoever things are just
Whatsoever things are pure
Whatsoever things are of good report
If there be any virtue, if there be any praise,
Think on these things."

-- Philippians, 4:8

Once in a Lifetime

## ABOUT THE AUTHOR

Barbara Fisk was born "a long time ago, in 1929." While growing up, her family lived in California, Oregon, Washington and Alaska, learning the joys of nature and outdoor living. Music was a major part of her life, as her father had a Master's degree in the subject. Both of her parents taught piano, violin, cello, and guitar.

School was not fun for her, and graduation day in 1947 was a blessing. Living in Alaska brought her many unusual experiences, and the best of all was meeting her future husband, who was on his way to join the Navy. Together they have memories of World War 2, Pearl Harbor, Vietnam, Korea, Desert Storm and the first hydrogen bomb tests. Eventually their family was increased to four with two children, and there was always a new adventure waiting.

As the years slipped by, Barbara discovered new pleasures such as learning to fly and oil painting, as well as the challenge of writing this book. One never knows what hidden talents they may have until they try!

www.ingramcontent.com/pod-product-compliance
Lightning Source LLC
Chambersburg PA
CBHW061201070526
44579CB00009B/92